T0065512

JONAH

Beyond the Whale

CHAD GROEN

WestBow
PRESS®
A DIVISION OF THOMAS NELSON
& ZONDERVAN

WestBow Press books may be ordered through booksellers or by contacting:

WestBow Press
A Division of Thomas Nelson & Zondervan
1663 Liberty Drive
Bloomington, IN 47403
www.westbowpress.com
844-714-3454

ISBN: 978-1-6642-2279-3 (sc)
ISBN: 978-1-6642-2278-6 (hc)
ISBN: 978-1-6642-2280-9 (e)

Library of Congress Control Number: 2021902387

Print information available on the last page.

WestBow Press rev. date: 03/03/2021

Contents

To my wife, Kristy, for supporting me
and encouraging me to publish this book.

Introduction

Jonah is a unique book in the Bible. Granted, every book in the Bible is unique in its own respectable way, but there are a lot of different elements that make Jonah an interesting, entertaining, and important book to read and study. Unfortunately, it's also a book that tends to get overlooked. A lot of people learn about the basic story of Jonah in Sunday school classes when they're kids, but when they grow up they become misled into thinking they know everything there is to know about the book—a guy gets swallowed by a fish, gets vomited out three days later, and converts a city. The story seems so simple and straightforward that they don't think there's any point in reading it or studying it. After all, it's a real short book with only four chapters that total forty-eight verses. They don't think there's anything else to learn about Jonah, so they assume that if they want to grow spiritually, they're better off focusing on other books in the Bible that they know have a lot of theological depth, like Psalms, Proverbs, the four Gospels (Matthew, Mark, Luke, and John), and some of the letters in the New Testament.

Does this mean the book of Jonah is not important and that it's okay to ignore it? Not at all! If you think Jonah is more of a kid-friendly story that's about a guy getting swallowed and vomited by a fish, then you need to take a closer look at this book—*much* closer look! There's a whole lot more to it than that.

It's more serious and important than you realize. Even though it's short, it's still loaded with useful information for people who want to learn more about God and also grow spiritually.

Even from a literary standpoint, the story of Jonah and its characters has a lot of depth. The story is unpredictable, and there are a lot of twists and turns. Even the ending is unpredictable.

To top it off, there are also a lot of connections that can be made between Jonah and the other books in the Bible. Even *Jesus* makes a connection between himself and Jonah. Recognizing those connections while reading this book can make it even more interesting and can also help emphasize the significance Jonah has among the other sixty-five books in the Bible.

The reason people didn't learn all this interesting and important information about Jonah when they were kids in Sunday school is simply because it would've been overwhelming for their young minds. The content was too theologically deep for them to understand, and there was too much information in the story for them to absorb. They can have fun learning about the very basic story of Jonah, but there's so much more to this book that makes it very important for teenagers and adults to read and study.

The bottom line is that the book of Jonah can't be overlooked by anyone, *even* if they think they know everything there is to know about the book.

On that note, *no* book in the Bible should be overlooked. The apostle Paul even says in 2 Timothy 3:16 that "All Scripture is God-breathed and is useful for teaching, rebuking, correcting and training in righteousness." Unfortunately, some books in the Bible tend to get overlooked, especially in the Old Testament, because Christians sometimes view certain books as being more resourceful than others. As a result, they spend a lot of time reading and studying those books and end up paying little to no attention to the rest of the Bible.

The reality is that each book in the Bible—all sixty-six of them—has its own important lessons that can be gained when we read and study them. They can each help us in our spiritual growth in their own unique and respectable way.

Jonah is no exception. It helps us better understand things such as what God is really like and how he wants us to live our lives. He loves all of us, wants what's best for all of us, and also wants all of us to be in a relationship with him. He doesn't play favorites. He has a specific plan for each of our lives, and as long as we obey his calling we'll live a life that satisfies him and is also satisfying for us. Despite our flaws, we can still serve him in amazing ways and accomplish things we wouldn't have thought were possible.

The one thing we can't do is ignore God or hide from him, which Jonah learns the hard way in this book. If we do that and try to do things on our own, we're going to encounter lots of problems with no way out, no matter how hard we try. Sometimes we'll end up failing so miserably we'll hit rock bottom and will have no choice but to turn to God for help. When we do, he'll greet us with open arms and will be excited we came back to him.

This is just a small sample of the many great things we can learn from the book of Jonah. Yes, kids may enjoy it, but teenagers and adults will gain so much more from it spiritually that they may end up enjoying it even more than kids do. All they need to do is take the time to read it and study it (which shouldn't be too hard to do, given how short it is).

That's the purpose of this book—to help people better understand the book of Jonah. It'll walk you through the book—chapter by chapter, verse by verse—and not only explain the story but also the symbolism in it, the lessons we can learn from it, and the connections it has with other books of the Bible. You may even be surprised by some of the information you learn about Jonah. For example, did you know that Jonah and the city of Nineveh each show up in other books in the Bible? Or that this story about Jonah has some connections with the stories about Jesus in the four Gospels? Or that Jonah converted more people in one setting than anyone else in human history?

You may be surprised by all the interesting and important pieces of information that can be found in the book of Jonah, and you may also be surprised by how much it can help you grow spiritually. This is definitely more than just a kid's story. It's the word of God. It was written a few thousand years ago, but it has stood the test of time for very good reasons. It's time to learn what those reasons are, because this is definitely not a book that can be ignored or taken lightly.

Even if you're already familiar with Jonah, it's possible there are elements in the book you're not aware of or that you may have forgotten about because you haven't read it in so long. It may be a short story, but it's jam-packed with significant information that God wants us to know about.

So let's dig in and see what all is in this unique book.

Some Background Information on the Book of Jonah

The minor prophet

The book of Jonah is considered to be the book of a "minor prophet," and it's located in a section of the Bible that includes all the minor prophetic books, starting with Daniel and ending with Malachi—the last book in the Old Testament. Don't let the term "minor prophet" fool you. It doesn't mean these books are less important than the other books in the Bible or that the prophets in those books, including Jonah, are less important than the other prophets in the Bible. Far from it! The term "minor prophet" simply means they're short books compared to the other prophetic books in the Old Testament. The other prophetic books are known as "major prophets," mainly because of how long they are (the longest is Isaiah, which is sixty-six chapters long). Since Jonah is only four chapters long, it's pretty obvious that it's short enough to be a minor prophet. But remember, Jonah is just as important as all the other books in the Bible.

Who wrote it?

It's unclear who wrote the book of Jonah, but it's traditionally believed to have been Jonah himself. There are several other books in the Bible in which the author is unknown, especially in the Old Testament, so this is not an unusual circumstance.

When was this book written?

It's estimated that this book was written sometime between AD 750 and 725. The fact that this book has stood the test of time and is still being read and studied by millions, if not billions, of people around the world after all these centuries is truly remarkable. Clearly, God was involved in preserving the contents of this book so it can always be available for people to read and study. For that matter, the same can easily be said about the other sixty-five books of the Bible.

CHAPTER 1

JONAH AND THE SAILORS

A little background information on Jonah

THE BOOK OF Jonah doesn't go into much detail on Jonah's background. In fact, the first verse of the book jumps right into the story. It says:

The word of the Lord came to Jonah son of Amittai.

That's all we learn about Jonah's background in this book—that he's the son of a man named Amittai. However, it's worth mentioning that this is *not* the first time we see Jonah in the Bible. He first shows up in 2 Kings 14:25 in an event that took place before the book of Jonah. This is part of a passage that is talking about the reign of Israel's king, Jeroboam, son of Jehoash.

Israel had many bad kings throughout the Old Testament, unfortunately, and Jeroboam was definitely one of them. Verse 24 of that passage even says he did "evil in the eyes of the Lord." However, there was at least one good thing he did during his reign, and it's stated in verse 25. He "restored the boundaries of Israel from Lebo Hamath to the Dead Sea in accordance with the word of the Lord, the God of Israel, spoken through his servant Jonah son of Amittai, the prophet from Gath Hepher." In other words, God sent Jonah to Jeroboam to deliver a message to him, and that message was for Jeroboam to restore those boundaries. Jonah was obedient to God by delivering that message as he was told, and Jeroboam took that message to heart.

So 2 Kings 14:25 gives us a little more information about Jonah: First of all, we learn that he's a prophet from a place called Gath Hepher.

Second, we learn he's an important prophet who is faithful to God. God gave him a very important message to deliver to King Jeroboam during a time of uncertainty for God's people. Here we are later on in the book of Jonah, and God is calling him for an even bigger mission.

Third, we learn that Jonah is obedient. He listened to God and followed through with his orders. When you consider that Jeroboam was powerful, corrupt, and disobedient toward God, it would've been easy for Jonah to chicken out and not go to Jeroboam. But that wasn't the case. Jonah did exactly as he was told, and as a result something very good happened: the border that separated Israel from their enemy nation Damascus was restored. This was very significant at the time, because Israel was dealing with some serious threats from Damascus.

Now God is calling Jonah for another mission. In verse 2, God tells him:

> Go to the great city of Nineveh and preach against it, because its wickedness has come up before me.

It's never a good thing when God has a prophet deliver that kind of message. The Bible talks about how God is omnipresent, which means everywhere all the time (Proverbs 15:3; Jeremiah 23:24); omniscient, which means all knowing (Psalms 139:4, 147:5; 1 John 3:20); omnipotent, which means all powerful (Daniel 4:35; Ephesians 1:19), and also jealous (Exodus 20:5; Deuteronomy 4:24). This means God can see everyone all the time and always knows what everyone is saying, doing, and thinking. He doesn't want you to ignore him or disobey him, and he doesn't want you to worship or idolize anyone or anything else but him. If you're sinning against him, he'll know about it immediately. He won't be happy about it, and he has the power to do something about it. He may not punish you like he sometimes did to the Israelites and their enemies throughout the Old Testament, but he will allow things to happen (or in some cases, allow things not to happen) that can make life difficult for you.

At the beginning of Jonah we see God threatening his wrath on Nineveh. Time and again throughout the Old Testament we see his wrath come down on those who kept sinning against him. It happens as early as the book of Genesis in the story of Noah, when God produced a massive flood that nearly wiped out every creature and human on earth (only Noah and his family survived, via the ark that God told them to build). Why did God do that? Because there was so much sin in the world that God actually regretted creating humans (Genesis 6:6). He was willing to kill them all off because of that, but there was one person with whom he found favor, so God allowed him and his family to live—that was Noah (Genesis 6:8), and it's pretty sad that he was the only person in the entire world who wasn't against God.

We also see God's wrath later in Genesis when he became so angry with the sins of Sodom and Gomorrah that he sent down fire on the two towns, killing and destroying everything in them.

We even see God's wrath toward his own people in Israel. Throughout the Old Testament we see them turn away from God and disobey him up to the point when he snaps and causes an array of bad things to happen to them. Their pain and suffering don't stop until they turn back to God for help and forgiveness. When they do, God relents and shows mercy and love to them again.

For some of these situations, God used prophets like Jonah to warn Israel and their kings to stop disobeying him and turn their hearts back to him. Unfortunately, the Israelites didn't always listen to the prophets and sometimes even rebuked the prophets, viewing them more as a nuisance or even as an enemy. As a result, they continued to live sinful lifestyles until God stepped in and wreaked havoc on their lives. He was doing what the prophets had warned the Israelites he would do to them until they refocused their lifestyles so that they were once again centered around God.

This jealousy of God probably doesn't make him sound like a nice person, but it's important to remember that not only did he create us, he also loves us and wants us to have a close and loving relationship with him. It's very rude and impolite to turn your back on him and sin against him. That would make anyone frustrated. God obviously needed to punish such people to remind them he still exists, to demonstrate how powerful he is, and to also show them how serious he is about loving us and wanting us to love him back.

Now God's wrath is stirring up again, and this time it's against one of Israel's enemies—Nineveh.

What's Nineveh?

A lot of people may not realize it, but this is actually not the first time the city of Nineveh shows up in the Bible. It first appears all the way back in Genesis 10:11–12. This chapter lists the descendants of Noah's three sons, Shem, Ham, and Japheth. In verse 9 we learn that one of Ham's descendants is Nimrod, and verses 10–12 go on to say that "the first centers of [Nimrod's] kingdom were Babylon, Uruk, Akkad and Kalneh, in Shinar. From that land he went to Assyria, where he built Nineveh, Rehoboth Ir, Calah and Resen, which is between Nineveh and Calah—which is the great city."

This means Nineveh had been around for a very long time—even longer than Israel. It was located in present-day Iraq, and eventually became the capital of Assyria. It was a flourishing city, but unfortunately, because it was part of Assyria during Jonah's time, the Ninevites were also enemies to the Israelites.

We also see the Nineveh mentioned later on, in 2 Kings 19:36. It shows up toward the end of a conflict between Judah's king, Hezekiah, and Assyria's king, Sennacherib. You can read about the conflict in 2 Kings 18–19 (the same story is told in Isaiah 36–37). To make a long story short, Sennacherib sends an army to Jerusalem to try to conquer the land, but then the angel of the Lord sweeps into the Assyrian camp one night and kills 185,000 men. After that, 2 Kings 19:36 says, "So Sennacherib king of Assyria broke camp and withdrew. He returned to Nineveh and stayed there" (this verse also shows up in Isaiah 37:37).

For many generations the Ninevites treated the Israelites very poorly, and they had no fear, respect, or belief in Israel's God. They had their own gods they believed in, worshipped, and prayed to, which meant they had their own religious practices and rules to live by, and they were completely different from Israel's. This all adds up to a very sinful nation, and Nineveh was like that for a very long time. Now God has had enough of Nineveh, and he wants Jonah to go there and preach against them.

Jonah's response

Given what little we know about Jonah so far, and also given how obedient and close to God the other prophets are in the Bible, you would think Jonah would immediately pack up his bags and head for Nineveh. You would think Jonah would be anxious to preach against them, since they had been a thorn in his nation's side for so many years, and now his almighty powerful God is angry with them. Unfortunately, Jonah doesn't do that. He does the complete opposite. Verse 3 says:

> *But Jonah ran away from the Lord and headed for Tarshish. He went down to Joppa, where he found a ship bound for that port. After paying the fare, he went aboard and sailed for Tarshish to flee from the Lord.*

Where's Tarshish?

Tarshish was located a long way west of Israel in present-day Spain, at the opposite end of the Mediterranean Sea. Nineveh, meanwhile, was located a long way *east* of Israel. In other words, Jonah fled in the opposite direction from where God wanted him to go. Tarshish was near the western end of the known world, which means Jonah tried to flee as far away from Nineveh as he possibly could.

We find out later why he fled, but Jonah's action is common in a lot of people today. They feel God calling them to do something, but they decide not to do it for a variety of reasons. They may be afraid of doing it, or they don't think they can afford it, they don't think they have the knowledge or expertise to pull it off, they don't want to change their current lifestyle, they want to wait and do it later in life, etc. This is not the attitude God wants us to have. When he calls us to do something, he wants us to act immediately. His plans for each of our lives are very unique, and we don't always know what the next part of his plan is going to be until he calls us to start moving in that direction. Jeremiah 29:11 even says, "'For I know the plans I have for you,' declares the Lord, 'plans to prosper you and not to harm you, plans to give you hope and a future.'"

On a brief side note, when the Bible promises that we'll prosper, that doesn't necessarily mean financially, which a lot of people in our society are inclined to think. Sometimes that's one of the ways in which we'll prosper, but that isn't always the case. The Bible means we'll prosper in more spiritual ways and mental ways, which can be more rewarding to us than anything else in the world. Sometimes it's hard to believe that until you experience it. When you do experience it, you won't desire anything else. You'll truly understand what it means to prosper, and you'll be so grateful that God allowed you to prosper.

We all play an integral part in shaping up this broken world that needs God's love and mercy. He wants us to serve him so we can grow closer to him and have a positive influence in the lives of others. When the timing is right, God will call us into action. When he does, we can't turn our backs on him and try to flee from his calling. That's not an option (some people think it is, but then they learn the hard way that it never was an option). God's going to keep nudging you until you obey and follow through with the plans he has for your life.

A big mistake people sometimes make is to think they can successfully avoid God or hide from him so they can do other things with their lives that seem more interesting or that they feel more comfortable doing. This is not possible, no matter how hard you try. Jonah thought he could pull it off by fleeing for Tarshish, but it didn't fool God at all. God knew what was happening (we mentioned earlier that he's omniscient—all knowing), and he didn't want Jonah to go to Tarshish. He was going to make sure that didn't happen, which is why verse 4 says:

Then the Lord sent a great wind on the sea, and such a violent storm arose that the ship threatened to break up.

What happens next is pretty interesting. There are other people on this ship, and they don't know anything about this conflict between Jonah and God. As a result, the sudden arrival of this "violent storm" was quite a surprise to them and an unpleasant one as well. It caused them to lose control of the ship, and now it's on the verge of getting devoured by this storm.

Also, they apparently didn't believe in Jonah's God—the one true God, *Yahweh* (that's the Hebrew name God wanted the Israelites to call him; it means *I am*). Instead, they each had their own god in whom they believed. We learn that in verse 5a, which says:

All the sailors were afraid and each cried out to his own god.

That obviously didn't work, because they were crying out to gods that didn't exist. They then tried other ways to keep the ship afloat. Verse 5b says:

And they threw the cargo into the sea to lighten the ship.

By this point it's obvious that things are getting real nasty, and that the sailors are panicking. They had sailed far enough away from the shore that they couldn't quickly turn back or even try swimming back (otherwise they probably wouldn't have panicked). They've lost control of their ship; it's stuck in the middle of the Great Sea—which is what the Mediterranean Sea was called back then—and this storm is on the verge of devouring them.

However, despite all this chaos, Jonah was completely oblivious to it. Verse 5c says:

> *But Jonah had gone below deck, where he lay down and fell into a deep sleep.*

First of all, this is somewhat ironic when you consider the fact that this storm was geared toward Jonah, and yet it's not waking him up, even though it's strong enough to destroy the ship. This storm was God's attempt to make Jonah go back to the mainland so he can travel to Nineveh, but he's the only one on the ship who hasn't even noticed the storm. This might look like a failure on God's part, but you'll find out later that he wanted this event to play out in this particular way.

How someone could sleep through all this chaotic noise and movement is somewhat baffling, but it's possible that God put Jonah in this deep sleep so he wouldn't notice the storm initially. In fact, Jonah's not the only person in the Bible whom we see sleeping through a big storm while at sea. It happens hundreds of years later, in a story in the New Testament, and the person sleeping through the storm is none other than Jesus Christ.

The story is documented in both Matthew 8:23–26 and Mark 4:35–39. Jesus and his disciples were boating across a lake when a "furious" storm swept in, terrifying his disciples. Jesus, however, was sleeping peacefully in the stern of the boat, completely oblivious to the storm. His disciples woke him up and begged him to calm the storm before it killed them. Jesus ended up doing just that, but he was disappointed in his disciples because of their lack of faith. Despite what was happening, they shouldn't have been afraid, because they knew that Jesus was with them; it didn't matter that he was asleep. Unfortunately, they hadn't fully understood yet who Jesus was and what he was capable of doing.

In the story of Jonah, the sailors had every right to be afraid. They had no clue what was going on, and there was no one on board who was capable of helping them. They were alone in the middle of the Mediterranean Sea with no way out of this violent storm.

Also, you'll notice that while Jonah was asleep, the sailors started calling out to their own gods for help and then started panicking when they realized those gods weren't responding. It's important to note that if Jonah hadn't fallen into a deep sleep, these sailors wouldn't have had an opportunity to experience such fear and helplessness, because Jonah would've had God calm the storm almost immediately. If that had happened, it might not have been obvious to the sailors that Jonah's God was the one who calmed the storm. They might've thought it was calmed by one of their own gods or that the storm went away on its own. However, it was important for them to experience fear and helplessness because it ends up playing a big factor in something they decide to do toward the end of this chapter.

It may not seem fair for them to be victims of God's wrath like this, especially since his wrath was geared toward Jonah. Granted, you can make the case that they deserved God's wrath because they were breaking the second commandment by believing in other gods. But they weren't doing anything wrong by setting out to sea themselves, and they had no idea Jonah was doing something wrong when they allowed him to tag along with them. However, later in this chapter you're going to see something amazing come out of this incident. The sailors don't realize it, but they're actually going to benefit from this storm in ways they would've never imagined.

The sailors became so scared and desperate for help that the captain finally woke Jonah up. Verse 6 says:

> *The captain went to him and said, 'How can you sleep? Get up and call on your god! Maybe he will take notice of us so that we will not perish.'*

Let's think about this for a moment. We live in an age in which people have a lot of disrespect and hatred toward other religions, and they don't want anything to do with them. This isn't too surprising, because some religions view the other religions as sinful and misleading and anyone who practices those other religions is the very image of sin and evil. This even leads to violence throughout the world between people of opposing religions. Some people have such negative views on religions outside of their own that they're willing to arrest, abuse, or sometimes even kill people who practice those other religions.

On that note, there are also some Christians, unfortunately, who are biased toward people from other religions. Yes, the Bible says we should not worship any other gods except God himself, but it also says we should love our neighbors as we love ourselves. Jesus even makes it clear in Matthew 22:37–39 that loving our neighbors is one of the two greatest commandments (the other is to love God). Unfortunately, some Christians don't fully understand that, and instead they think it's justified to look down on other religions. In fact, there are some who even look down on other Christians simply because their church is of a different denomination. This only adds to the divisions and conflicts that plague our world today.

However, these sailors in Jonah 1 were nothing like that. They were not stubborn or closed-minded about their religious beliefs. They showed no hatred or disrespect toward those who believed in other gods. In fact, they were even willing to put their trust in another God, one that none of them had called out to yet. They knew Jonah served a different God than they did and that he hadn't called out to his God for help. Maybe if Jonah called out to that God, he would actually listen and show mercy by helping them. They were desperate to get out of this storm alive and were willing to try something different.

The bottom line is that these sailors were willing to make a leap of faith by trusting in a foreign God they hadn't believed in before and probably were unfamiliar with. If you want to put your faith in God, you need to be willing to make a leap of faith. Faith that God created everything including you; faith that he's in control of everything and is there to help if you call to him; faith that he sent his only son Jesus to earth to show us how to live our lives; faith that he sacrificed Jesus on a cross to bear the punishment for all our sins; faith that Jesus rose from the grave three days after his death and is now seated at the right hand of God in heaven; and faith that someday, when you die, you'll be united with him in heaven and will be there for all eternity.

For some, this is a more difficult commitment to make than others, which can be understandable for a multitude of reasons. But you need to push yourself to throw out any fear, doubt, and concern you may have, so you can step forward into the glorious light of almighty God and walk along the path he has chosen for you to live—a path that gives you hope and allows you to prosper.

If you do that you won't have any regrets about your decision, especially in the long run. You may encounter a few bumps along the road, but they won't be too big for you to handle with God's help. Also, you'll be eternally rewarded in amazing ways that are beyond comprehension. If these sailors can do it, then you can do it, too!

However, at this moment in the story of Jonah, it wasn't obvious to the sailors that Jonah's God was the one they needed to trust and call upon. You'll notice in verse 7 that Jonah doesn't even call to God after the captain told him to do that (this isn't surprising, since Jonah's trying to run away from God). This means the sailors are still struggling to figure out what, if anything, can be done to survive this vicious storm. Verse 7 says:

> *Then the sailors said to each other, 'Come, let us cast*
> *lots to find out who is responsible for this calamity.'*
> *They cast lots and the lot fell on Jonah.*

Casting lots was a common practice for centuries, and there are other stories in the Bible in which you see people casting lots. People did it to help make big decisions or find answers to questions they were struggling with. In this situation, the sailors were struggling to figure out why this fearsome storm suddenly came upon them and was threatening their lives. They seemed to believe that someone on board the ship was responsible for this, and that this was a form of punishment from that person's god for something he did. They had no clue which person it was, so they decided to cast lots to figure out who should be blamed.

It's safe to assume that God was in control of this lot when it was cast, because it ended up pointing right to Jonah. It's only fair that this would happen because, after all, Jonah was the reason God created this storm. At this moment Jonah was probably starting to realize that God was behind these recent events. God obviously didn't want him to go to Tarshish, so he made it loud and clear that he knew what Jonah was doing and that he didn't approve of Jonah's actions. God wanted him to turn around and go to Nineveh. It's no coincidence the lot fell to Jonah.

To us, casting lots may seem like nothing but luck. But back then there were a lot of people who took it very seriously, and these sailors were some of those people. You'll notice they didn't seem to care much about Jonah until after the lot fell to him. After that they became very curious about him, because they assumed the lot to be true and accurate, that it had for sure shown them who was to blame for this life-threatening situation they were in. There was a whole lot more to Jonah than they realized. He wasn't some average Joe wanting to take a trip to Tarshish.

So, just like that, Jonah became the center of attention on this ship, and the sailors started demanding answers from him. Verses 8–10 say:

> So they asked him, 'Tell us, who is responsible for making all this trouble for us? What kind of work do you do? Where do you come from? What is your country? From what people are you?' He answered, 'I am a Hebrew and I worship the Lord, the God of heaven, who made the sea and the dry land.' This terrified them and they asked, 'What have you done?' (They knew he was running away from the Lord because he had already told them so.)

Things are starting to fall into place for the sailors. Now they know why this storm has shown up and is devouring their ship. They realize it's Jonah's God, Yahweh, who created the storm and that he's obviously mad at Jonah for running away. The only problem is that, although they've found the cause of this storm, they have yet to find a solution for how to survive it.

Verse 11 says:

> The sea was getting rougher and rougher. So they asked him, 'What should we do to you to make the sea calm down for us?'

Unfortunately for these sailors, they got stuck in the middle of this conflict simply because they were in the wrong place at the wrong time. Some might be tempted to believe that God was threatening all their lives because he was mad at them for not believing in him and believing in other gods instead (which is a violation of the second commandment). However, that's not what God's anger was focused on right then. His anger was focused solely on one person on that ship who disobeyed him. Unfortunately, that person was also one of his own people, Jonah. The sailors on that ship just happened to be victims of God's wrath as a result of Jonah's disobedience.

It's possible Jonah was hoping the sailors would outlast this storm so he could continue on to Tarshish, away from Nineveh. However, it's now obvious that that's not going to happen. God isn't going to be denied, and he's making sure Jonah doesn't get any further away from Nineveh than he already has. If Jonah thought he could escape God, he was very wrong, and he learned it the hard way.

Jonah realizes these sailors have lost control of the ship and can't even turn around to head back the way they came. It becomes obvious to him that he only has two options: one is to stay on the ship, which means the storm will continue and soon destroy the ship, killing him and everyone else on it; the other option is for him to do something he probably doesn't like but would spare the ship and the sailors on it. That's the option he goes with, because in verse 12 he tells the sailors:

> 'Pick me up and throw me into the sea,' he replied, 'and it will become calm. I know that it is my fault that this great storm has come upon you.'

At this point you would think the sailors would be willing to do anything right then and there to stop the storm, but throwing Jonah into this violent sea was where they drew the line. They were nowhere near land, and the water was so rough from the storm that they knew Jonah would die if they threw him in there. They obviously didn't want someone's blood on their hands, so they decided to try getting out of this mess on their own. Verse 13 says:

Instead, the men did their best to row back to land. But they could not, for the sea grew even wilder than before.

This is a big mistake a lot of people make. They think they can do things on their own, without God's help, but what they don't realize is that they're setting themselves up for failure when they do that. Things may work out okay for a little while, but eventually they'll run into some problems—they'll encounter their own "storm," so to speak—and sometimes even dig themselves a really big hole. They'll then try to resolve the issue(s) on their own, but it still won't work no matter how hard they try. It isn't until they seek God's help that things start to get better and the storm calms down.

Unfortunately, it isn't always easy for people to turn to God when they need his help. Some people are selfish enough that they don't like help from others—they're convinced they can figure things out on their own—and some just don't feel comfortable doing what needs to be done to get the help they need, such as checking into rehab, going to counseling, or turning their back on some friends who are a bad influence and looking for new friends who are a good influence. Whatever the situation is, people don't always like the solution God provides them. However, they need to understand that things will not get better for them—and sometimes things will even get worse—until they finally give in and accept the help God is providing them. In the long run they'll be glad they gave in and did what God was calling them to do. Sometimes they'll even regret how long it took them to start obeying God.

Unfortunately, there will still be moments in life when you encounter issues while being obedient to God. This doesn't mean you're doing something wrong or that you need to give up. You need to persevere through those difficulties while continuing to seek God's help (and you can seek his help through prayer and reading your Bible). If you can do that, he'll help you succeed in amazing ways (1 Timothy 4:16). It might not happen instantly, but you'll eventually notice that things are gradually getting better and better if you continue to persevere. That experience can help you grow in many ways, and in the end God will reward you for the good things you were able to accomplish (Romans 5:3–5 and Hebrews 10:36).

In fact, James 1:2–4 even says that it's good when we encounter difficulties in life. It's not fun when it happens, but if we persevere and stay faithful to God, it will help us grow closer to him and make us more "mature" (see also Romans 5:3–5).

The bottom line is that when we need God's help, we can't ignore him and try to fix things on our own. We need to seek his help and understand that he knows what's best for us. He'll point us in the right direction, and we need to trust him and pursue that path, knowing he's in the process of getting us out of the giant hole we've dug ourselves into.

The sailors found themselves in that position. They thought they could get out of this storm on their own without doing what God wanted them to do. Instead, things only got worse, and they finally reached a point in which they realized their only option was to obey Jonah's God. That meant they had to throw Jonah into the raging sea. They obviously didn't feel comfortable doing this, though, because verse 14 says:

*Then they cried out to the Lord, 'Please, Lord, do
not let us die for taking this man's life. Do not hold
us accountable for killing an innocent man, for you,
Lord, have done as you pleased.'*

On a side not, it's kind of funny that they considered Jonah to
be an "innocent" man when they knew he had disobeyed his own
God, and they could clearly see God's wrath coming down on all
of them as a result of that sin. If Jonah were an "innocent" man,
he wouldn't have committed that sin. The reality is that Jonah is
far from innocent; he clearly has sinned against God, and now
God is punishing him for it.

Verses 15–16 say:

*Then they took Jonah and threw him overboard,
and the raging sea grew calm. At this the men greatly
feared the Lord, and they offered a sacrifice to the
Lord and made vows to him.*

A moment ago, these sailors were very reluctant to throw
Jonah off the ship, which was what God wanted them to do. By
the time they finally did it, they witnessed Jonah's God doing
exactly what Jonah said he'd do (which was a lot more than
what their own gods had done during that storm), and it caused
them to have a change of heart. They probably even thought to
themselves, "Why didn't we throw him in sooner?" (no offense to
Jonah). They hadn't realized how much better things were going
to get, and were probably surprised not only at how simple the
solution was but also at how quickly things got better.

Sometimes our issues can get resolved quickly like that when
we turn to God. Other times it takes more time and effort because
of how big or numerous our issues are, but God will still guide
us through in the best way possible. Don't give up, though, if it

turns out to be a slow process. God is still at work in getting you out of your mess. Just stay patient, keep persevering, and keep trusting God. He'll get you out eventually, and no other method will work as well as his.

To make things even better for the sailors, not only were their lives saved but they also came to know God and put their faith in him. Remember when these sailors were calling out to other gods for help because they believed in those gods and thought those gods would save them. Now they've learned there's only one God who answers prayer, and he's always there for you whenever you need him.

The good thing that came out of this situation

It's also worth pointing out that if Jonah had never betrayed God, he never would have encountered these sailors, and it's possible these sailors never would have come to know God. This is a situation we see a lot, not only in the Bible but also in our own lives and in the lives of others. Sometimes, when something bad happens, God can turn it into a good thing.

A biblical example of this is the story of Joseph from the book of Genesis. Making a long story short, Joseph's brothers hated him, so they sold him into slavery in Egypt. The next several years were very rough for Joseph, until one day Pharaoh was told that there was a man named Joseph who was good at interpreting dreams. Pharaoh had recently had a couple of bizarre dreams that were troubling him, and no one was able to interpret them for him. He then asked Joseph, and not only was Joseph able to interpret them—that the next seven years would be great for harvesting the land, but then it would be followed by seven really bad years due to a severe drought that was going to hit the land—but Pharaoh grew to like him so much that he made Joseph his right-hand man. Suddenly Joseph went from rock bottom to being the second-most powerful person in all of Egypt. With this power, he was able to rescue his family from that severe drought. Had Joseph's brothers not sold him into slavery, he would've continued to live with his family and they all would've died from the drought.

Keep in mind that they were descendants of Abraham, and God had told Abraham his descendants would be as "numerous as the stars (Genesis 22:17)" and would also become a great nation (Genesis 12:2). That almost didn't happen because of the drought, but God had made it possible by having Joseph sold into slavery many years earlier. This is why, in Genesis 50:20, Joseph tells his brothers, "You intended to harm me, but God intended it for good to accomplish what is now being done."

Another biblical example, and undoubtedly the biggest one of all, is something that happened to our Lord and Savior Jesus Christ. He was wrongfully accused, tortured, and hung to die on a cross. He never sinned during his time on Earth, so he didn't deserve the harsh punishment that was inflicted on him. What happened to him was very wrong and unfair, but God made something truly amazing come out of this tragic event. When Jesus died, he served as a sacrifice for us so we can be saved from all our sins and have an opportunity to spend eternity with him in heaven. After his death he even rose from the dead and later on went up to heaven to prepare a place for those who acknowledge him as their Lord and Savior. This great opportunity came out of something really bad that had happened to Jesus.

Even in our own lives, there are times when something bad happens to us, but it ends up leading to something good that may not have happened otherwise. You may be late for work because of car problems, but if you had left at your normal time you would've been hit by someone running a red light. You may flunk a course in college and have to take it again, but while taking it a second time you meet a woman in the class who you start dating and eventually marry. Or you may fail to get a job you really wanted, but that company goes out of business a year later. You may get a job you weren't as interested in, but you end up meeting someone there who you become good friends with, and he ends up bringing you to Christ. The examples are endless.

This first chapter of Jonah fits right in with these examples. Jonah did a bad thing by fleeing for Tarshish, but it resulted in something good happening that he likely wasn't expecting: these sailors came to know God. Had Jonah obeyed God, he would never have gone near that ship, and those sailors wouldn't have come to know God. They likely would've had a peaceful trip to Tarshish, but it's also possible they would never have received any other opportunities to experience God's presence, power, and mercy, which means they would've continued to live in sin by believing in false gods.

Does this mean it's okay to sin or to allow something bad to happen to you?

Not at all! If you really love God, who created you and loves you (the first commandment even states you should love him), you won't want to disobey him by sinning against him. You'll want to serve him and will want to do everything for his glory so he may be pleased by your efforts and accomplishments. That's also what he wants you to do. You may encounter problems along the way, but don't worry if that happens. God is still with you to help you. If you persevere and work hard to get out of a bad situation while seeking God's help, he'll help you get out of it, and that experience will build you up spiritually.

Also, if you just allow bad things to happen to you, it's going to really make life more difficult and burdensome than necessary. You're likely not going to be as grateful for your life as God would like you to be, and you probably won't be able to serve God as well as he'd like.

This event with Jonah and the sailors, along with the examples we mentioned earlier—Joseph becoming Pharaoh's right-hand man and Jesus dying on the cross—are evidence that God is always in control, that everything happens at the time he wants, and that events happen in a way in which the end result can be amazingly positive. It's no coincidence these sailors started believing in God after the storm went away. God planned that to happen. He used Jonah's shortcoming to make himself known to these sailors. During the storm, those sailors thought they were in the wrong place at the wrong time, and were probably wishing they'd left Jonah on the dock when they set sails for Tarshish. The reality is they were actually in the *right* place at the *right* time. It was God's timing for them to be saved, both physically and spiritually. He saved their physical bodies from the storm, and he also saved their souls from their sins.

The next time you encounter a "storm" in your life, don't worry. God is there to help you get out of it. All you have to do is seek him (Matthew 7:7–8 and Luke 11:9–10). Also, don't be surprised if something good comes from that storm. It won't be a coincidence; it'll be part of God's plan.

What happens afterward to the sailors?

We never see or hear about those sailors again in the book of Jonah. We don't know whether or not they continued to believe in God for the rest of their lives or whether or not they still believed in any of those other gods to whom they called out earlier, but we know that they at least came to know the one true God and started praising him and trusting him. It's obvious they're in good shape on their ship now that the storm has dissipated. The end of this chapter has a happy ending for them, but it's the complete opposite for Jonah. He was just thrown off the boat while the storm was still raging, and after that, verse 17 says:

Now the Lord provided a huge fish to swallow Jonah, and Jonah was in the belly of the fish three days and three nights.

The storm has calmed down and the sailors are happily praising God, but Jonah meanwhile is trapped inside a fish and is obviously in a lot of trouble. What's really sad is that he got himself into this trouble. God told him to do something and he chose not to. Now he's paying the price in a big way. He could've easily avoided this if he would've obeyed God in the first place.

This is what happens when we try to avoid God. We go our own way, try to do things ourselves, and eventually we run into a bunch of trouble that could've easily been avoided if we would've obeyed his calling. We can encounter many issues—or one huge issue—that make us feel trapped with no way out, like we're stuck in the belly of a fish. Jonah tried to avoid God, and it led to him getting trapped with no way out. It was a huge mistake on his part, and we need to learn from it.

Was Jonah really in that fish for three days and three nights?

Unfortunately, this is where some people question whether the story of Jonah is true or fictitious. People know it would be impossible for Jonah to remain alive inside the belly of a fish— or any animal for that matter—for three days and three nights without dying or being digested. It's safe to assume that at least some of the events in the book of Jonah really happened, but this event, with Jonah being stuck inside a fish for so long and surviving it, seems too far-fetched and unrealistic for some people to believe.

One could argue that this part of the story is metaphorical—a symbolical way of demonstrating things like how angry God was with Jonah, how rough our lives can become when we ignore God, and how he's always there to help us when we call to him. However, when you look at all the unexplainable miracles God performs throughout the Bible and take into consideration the many passages that talk about how powerful God is, it's safe to assume that he was in complete control of this situation and, through his mercy and awesome power, allowed Jonah to stay alive inside that fish for three days and three nights.

Regardless, this is how chapter 1 ends. It's the longest chapter of the book at 17 verses, and it ends with a big cliffhanger—Jonah is now trapped in the belly of a fish in the Mediterranean Sea, and things aren't looking good for him at all.

CHAPTER 2

JONAH AND THE FISH

CHAPTER 2 BEGINS right where the first chapter left off. It says in verse 1:

> *From inside the fish Jonah prayed to the Lord his God.*

This chapter is only 10 verses long, and verses 2–9 make up Jonah's prayer. This chapter tends to get overlooked when people talk about the story of Jonah. That's understandable, because it seems like there's very little that actually happens in this chapter—it consists mainly of Jonah's prayer, and there isn't any plot progression until the last verse. However, it's still a pivotal moment in the story. You learn some new things about both Jonah and God, and Jonah also realizes he needs to stop running from God and start obeying him.

A prayer or a psalm?

If you're familiar with the book of Psalms, you may think that Jonah's prayer in this chapter sounds similar to some of the Psalms. That's understandable; there are a lot of lines in this prayer that can be found in various Psalms. This is probably not a coincidence. The Psalms had already been written, and in some cases also sung, well before Jonah's time, and as one of God's prophets, Jonah was familiar with the scriptures that had already been written at that point. It's possible he was thinking about some of those Psalms at this moment of fear, desperation, and hopelessness, when he needed God the most and was praying to him for help (after all, he had just been thrown into a violent sea and swallowed by a giant fish).

Jonah's prayer begins in verse 2:

> *He said: In my distress I called to the Lord, and he answered me. From deep in the dead I called for help, and you listened to my cry.*

Jonah is referring to what just happened to him. What's interesting is that the first line is word for word what David said in Psalm 18:6, "In my distress I called to the Lord." It's possible Jonah thought of this verse and realized it now applied to him in a way that was similar to David. Regardless, Jonah goes on to explain that he was on the verge of death (that's what he means when he says, "from deep in the realm of the dead") when he called to God for help. He had been thrown into the sea and knew he wasn't going to last much longer. He also knew God was capable of saving him—in fact, there was nothing else that *could* save him at this point—so he called out to God. Not only did God hear him, but he also answered his prayer.

The symbolism here is similar to what we discussed in chapter 1, that when we're in trouble and it seems that all hope is lost, we need to call out to God for help, because he's the only one we can trust to help us. It happened to the sailors in chapter 1, and now it's happening to Jonah here in chapter 2. It's not a good idea to wait until the last minute or until after you've hit rock bottom to call to him for help; unfortunately, we sometimes do that because we don't think it necessary to call to him sooner.

In fact, sometimes we don't even think about God until after we run into a bunch of trouble and need his help. That's not a good mindset at all. God is not someone who sits around waiting for people to pray to him for help. He wants to be in a relationship with us. We should always stay close to him and always communicate with him. We can't just use him as our own personal bailer when life gets difficult and then ignore him when life is going well. He wants a much closer relationship than that. He can also help us make better choices in life when we listen and obey him on a regular basis, including when life seems like it's working out well.

Verse 3 says:

> *You hurled me into the depths, into the very heart of the seas, and the currents swirled about me; all your waves and breakers swept over me.*

First of all, the part of this sentence that says, "all your waves and breakers swept over me," has almost the exact same wording as Psalm 42:7. Second, you'll notice at the beginning of this verse that Jonah says God "hurled" him into the sea. This is interesting, because it was the sailors who threw him into the sea in the previous chapter (verse 15), not God. The reason Jonah says that is because he knows that God was controlling the situation, that it was God's will for Jonah to be thrown into the sea, and that

God used the sailors to throw Jonah in. The sailors didn't really have much of a choice when they did that—it was either throw him in and hope God saves them, as Jonah said would happen, or leave him on board, which was a guarantee that the ship would be devoured by the storm and they would all die. They ended up doing what God wanted them to do. God was responsible for Jonah's getting thrown overboard.

In other words, the sailors were fulfilling God's will when they threw Jonah overboard. It's probably safe to assume they didn't realize they were doing that. They were trying to survive the storm and were told by Jonah that that was their only option. They probably figured Jonah was being punished for his disobedience. They had no idea they had become involved in a significant story, that not only were they helping God but the outcome of this situation would lead to them coming to know God and to fear him.

Sometimes our lives can have moments like this as well. We'll end up doing something briefly for someone, and it'll end up having a significant impact on their life; yet we don't always realize it, because we're not around them to witness it. We can do something that impacts a person we briefly meet in a store or restaurant and never find out about how rewarding that moment was for them. We can do something that impacts a co-worker or friend at school, but then we lose touch with them and never see or hear about the positive impact we had on their life. Regardless of the situation, God can use each of us to help others in many different ways, and we're not always aware of it. All these positive influences will be made known to us, though, when we're in heaven someday. God will be proud of us in how we served him and will tell us, "Well done, my good and faithful servant" (Luke 19:17).

We also learn in verse 3 that the sea was very rough for Jonah after he was thrown into it ("the currents swirled about me; all your waves and breakers swept over me"). Remember, this storm was created by God. He was making things really difficult for Jonah, so that Jonah would have no choice but to turn back to God. God sometimes does this to us in our own lives when we've been neglecting him, because he's trying to get us to turn our hearts back to him. Jonah seems to recognize this is an act of God, because he refers to the waves and breakers of the sea as "your" waves and breakers, meaning *God's* waves and breakers. This storm and the rapid currents weren't caused by random acts of nature; they were purposefully caused by God.

Verse 4 says:

> *I said, 'I have been banished from your sight; yet I*
> *will look again toward your holy temple.'*

You can find a similar saying in Psalm 5:7. Jonah has made it clear he's going to stop running from God and will turn his heart toward him. It's great that he's making the right decision to repent, but what's sad is that this is a recurring theme throughout the Old Testament for God's people, the Israelites. The reason it's sad is because this issue happens a lot with them, and it's always preceded by them sinning against God.

The Old Testament has a lot of stories of the Israelites choosing to neglect God and focus their hearts on other things. This causes them to sin in a variety of ways without feeling guilty about it. As time goes by, God becomes really disgusted with the neglect and the sinful lifestyles they've adopted, and he ends up sending calamity on them, causing them to suffer greatly. During their suffering, they turn back to God, repent of their sins, and call to him for help. God then rescues them from their troubles, and their relationship is restored. However, as time goes by, the

Israelites slowly turn their hearts away from God again, adopting sinful lifestyles again. God once again becomes so angry about this that he makes them suffer, forcing them to turn back to him again, repent of their sins, and cry for help. God helps them again, and the Israelites seem like they've learned from their mistakes. Instead, the cycle ends up repeating itself again and again.

This cycle continues throughout the Old Testament, and we see it happening here with Jonah. Jonah turned his back on God, then God caused him to suffer, and now Jonah is turning back to God. Jonah realizes he has made a mistake, and now he wants to make things right with God. It's very symbolic of the history of his people, the Israelites.

We sometimes see this happen in our own lives too. If we start ignoring God and do whatever we feel like without having any regrets about the sins we're committing, eventually God is going to create a storm too big for us to handle. We're going to encounter a lot of trouble, and the only way out will be to turn back to God and start obeying him again.

Verse 5 says:

> *The engulfing waters threatened me, the deep surrounded me; seaweed was wrapped around my head.*

It's hard to tell if Jonah means literally, metaphorically, or both, that the seaweed is "wrapped" around his head. Either way, this verse emphasizes the image of him being surrounded and trapped, with no way out under his own power. We see similar language used in Psalm 69:1–2 and Lamentations 3:54.

Things continue to look grim for Jonah. The first sentence of verse 6 says:

To the roots of the mountains I sank down; the earth beneath barred me in forever.

It seems there's no hope left for Jonah. He has sunk deep beneath the water, his life has hit rock bottom, both literally and metaphorically, and it's all because he turned his back on God and tried to do his own thing. As a result, he's now trapped, with no way out. His sin has messed up his life, and it looks like it's also going to cost him his life. Given how he disobeyed God—and you'd think he would've known better not to do that, considering he's a veteran prophet of God—it seems like it's only appropriate for Jonah's life to end like this.

When you think about it, this is what we all deserve, because of how sinful we all are. We all deserve to be cast away from God, to drown in our sins, and suffer God's wrath for being so sinful and so rebellious toward him. Romans 3:23 even says, "for all have sinned and fall short of the glory of God."

However, that's only half the story. There's a second sentence in Jonah 6:2 that's also important to know:

But you, Lord my God, brought my life up from the pit.

Despite all Jonah had done, God still reached out and saved him. It's worth pointing out that the word "pit" in this verse means *grave*. In other words, God saved Jonah from death. He did it by sending a fish to swallow Jonah so that he wouldn't drown. Likewise for us, God saved us from spiritual death, and he did it by sacrificing his son Jesus on the cross so we can all be saved from our sins and can all be given an opportunity to have eternal life with him in heaven. Romans 3:24 even says, "and all are justified freely by his grace through the redemption that came by Christ Jesus."

Why would God save us when we're constantly sinning against him?

This is a good question, and the answer is quite simple: God loves us. He wants us to be in a relationship with him. John 3:16 even says, "For God so loved the world that he gave his one and only Son, that whoever believes in him shall not perish but have eternal life." This is why God kept showing mercy to the Israelites throughout the Old Testament, despite the fact that they frequently sinned against him, and it's also why he showed mercy toward Jonah in this story, despite the fact that Jonah disobeyed him. The Israelites cried out to God for help, and he stepped in and saved them out of his love for them. Now Jonah has cried out to God for help, and he has stepped in and saved Jonah, via the fish, out of love for him.

God will do the same for you if you call out to him. He'll step in and help you out of his love for you. No matter what you do, his love for you will always be deeply rooted (Romans 5:5). He's the only one we can trust to always love us. No one else in this world can love us as much or as consistently.

In verse 7, Jonah says:

> When my life was ebbing away, I remembered you, Lord, and my prayer rose to you, to your holy temple.

First of all, you'll notice a similar saying in Psalm 18:6. Second, before God sent that fish to rescue Jonah, Jonah says at the beginning of this verse that he was on the verge of dying. You'll notice that it wasn't until *after* he prayed to God for help that God used the fish to rescue him. God wants us to always rely on him. In fact, he wants our lives to revolve around him, not the other way around. As a result, he won't normally help us unless our hearts are humbly focused on glorifying him.

Verse 8 says:

> *Those who cling to worthless idols turn away from*
> *God's love for them.*

This is a strong statement Jonah makes. First of all, we know it's a sin to "cling" to idols. Even though God didn't specifically use that term when he gave Moses the Ten Commandments, he definitely implied it in at least three of his commandments: the second commandment, "You shall have no other gods before me" (Exodus 20:3); the third commandment, "You shall not make for yourself an image in the form of anything in heaven above or on the earth beneath or in the waters below. You shall not bow down to them or worship them ..." (verses 4–5); and the tenth commandment, which is, in short, you should not "covet" anything (verse 17).

Idols can come in many forms. In the Bible we see people worshipping statues and other objects designed to represent gods that people believed existed in those days. We may not see idols like that today in our society, but we see them in many other forms that distract us from God. Idols come in a variety of forms like money, sports, video games, social media, music, TV, drugs, drinking, gambling, porn, etc. Some of these aren't necessarily sinful, but they all have the potential to consume our minds and become more important to us than God. If you're not making time for God because you're more interested in something else or because you feel like something else is more important than God, then that means that that particular item has become an idol to you. The one thing these "idols" have in common is that they're all earthly materials; they're part of this world, and we can't take them with us to heaven. It's not good to become too preoccupied with them. If you do, they'll cause you to ignore God.

God admits in Exodus 20:5 that he's a jealous God, so he wants our attention all the time. He wants us to focus our hearts and our lives around him, not on these earthly materials. In Colossians 3:2–3, Paul says, "set your hearts on things above, where Christ is seated … Not on earthly things." When we "cling" to these idols—these earthly materials—we turn away from God's love for us. God loves us deeply (so much he sacrificed his only son so we can be saved from our sins), but when we devote our lives to these earthly materials, we're not experiencing his love. Instead, we're turning our backs on him and ignoring his love, mercy, and calling. That's not at all what God wants us to do.

It's important to remember that these earthly materials are only temporary. They won't last forever. Some of them will fade away while we're still alive; others might still be around when we die, but they'll stay behind on earth when we go to the afterlife. They won't increase our chances of going to heaven, and they also won't earn us any special rewards in heaven.

In fact, no idol can give us the full satisfaction that we hope or expect it will. They might give us *some* satisfaction, but this will only last a short while, and then we'll find ourselves trying once again to fulfill the cravings of our minds and bodies. The problem is that it'll always be a losing battle, no matter how hard we try.

The only thing that can fully satisfy us is God's love, and it's an everlasting satisfaction that will never fail us or disappoint us. If you don't feel like his love is satisfying you, then that probably means you haven't actually experienced it yet. You need to pray for the Holy Spirit to open your heart and mind and to also guide you through your life so you can experience God's love and the amazing, never-ending satisfaction that comes with it.

It's important to remember we're all going to die someday, so at some point we're going to be permanently separated from these earthly materials. That doesn't mean we should spend a lot of time immersed in them while we're still on this earth. If we do that, then we're not going to be able to serve God and live our lives the way he wants, and he's not going to be happy about that. We'll also experience a lesser amount of satisfaction in our lives, because no matter how hard or how long we try, those idols will not satisfy us as much as God's love. That's why it's so important we don't let them deceive us or tempt us.

Imagine someone you love and want to spend a lot of time with, and you know they'll really enjoy it. But they keep ignoring you because they're more interested in doing something else that they think will give them more satisfaction, like golfing, playing video games, or going to a casino. It becomes very frustrating, because you want to be in a close relationship, but they don't realize how much more fun they'll have with you. In hindsight, that's similar to what God experiences with us when we "cling" to idols. We ignore him and focus more on those idols. It's not good for us to do that. We need to focus our lives on serving God, praying to him, praising him, and showing our love for him. That's what Jonah realizes he needs to do at this point in the book of Jonah, and now that's also what he *wants* to do. He proudly proclaims that in verse 9 when he says:

> But I, with shouts of grateful praise, will sacrifice
> to you. What I have vowed I will make good. I will
> say, "Salvation comes from the Lord."

He's not going to be like those who "cling" to idols and turn their backs on God. Instead, he's going to run *toward* God and do what God wanted him to do in the first place—go to Nineveh and preach against it.

That's what we *all* should do. We should never put idols in front of God. In fact, it's not even possible to have both God and idols as the main focus in our lives. There isn't room for both of them. God is jealous and wants to be the only focus in our lives. We have to choose one over the other: either God's love (a heavenly and eternal focus) or the materials of this world (a temporary and sinful focus that causes separation between us and God). We're a lot better off choosing God. That's the decision Jonah makes in this verse. Unfortunately, God had to cause all this turmoil in Jonah's life to help him realize that siding with God is the wiser choice to make.

Sometimes God has to do that in our own lives to help us realize we need to start following him. It's not always fun when that happens, because it can mess up our lives or make us feel embarrassed or vulnerable, but it's a good wakeup call that we need to change the way we live our lives. In the long run, you'll be glad he did that to you.

After praying on all this, Jonah learned his lesson. His heart was now in the right place, and he was ready to serve God. God ended up showing mercy toward him and answered his prayer in a miraculous way. Verse 10 says:

> And the Lord commanded the fish, and it vomited
> Jonah onto dry land.

Jonah survived the storm, the sea, and the three-day stay in the belly of the fish, and was delivered back to land safely. God was responsible for all of this. He was with Jonah the entire time. He helped Jonah recognize the mistake he'd made, he showed mercy toward Jonah, and he also guided Jonah to where he needed to be so he could stay alive and fulfill his calling.

God may have forgiven Jonah for his sin, but Jonah still had work that God wanted him to do. We find out what happens in the next chapter.

CHAPTER 3

JONAH AND THE NINEVITES

KEEP IN MIND that when the books of the Bible were written, there were no chapters, verses, or subheadings in them. Those were included centuries later to help organize the contents in each book and make them easier for people to read and find what they're looking for. Although this can be very helpful, it can sometimes be misleading when reading a story in the Bible. The reader will get to the end of a chapter and assume that means there's a break in the story, but that's not always the case. We see a good example of that at the end of Jonah 2. When you finish reading that chapter and begin reading chapter 3, you may get the impression that there's a gap of time in the story between these two chapters—maybe an hour, twelve hours, twenty-four hours, or possibly even more. That's not the case here. This book was written as one continuous story with no break in the action. In other words, as soon as you finish reading the last sentence in chapter 2, you're supposed to continue by reading the first sentence in chapter 3, because that scene hasn't ended yet.

Jonah had just been vomited out of the fish and onto dry land. It's possible God gave him a brief moment to recuperate from what he'd just been through—getting thrown overboard and then eaten and trapped inside the belly of a fish for three days and three nights—but God's not going to let him relax and get comfortable and lazy; Jonah is still on a mission from God, and God is still waiting for him to follow through. He even reminds Jonah in 3:1–2 what that mission is because it's time for Jonah to finally start working on it:

> *Then the word of the Lord came to Jonah a second time: 'Go to the great city of Nineveh and proclaim to it the message I give you.'*

If you think these first two verses of chapter 3 sound familiar, that's because they're very similar to the first two verses of chapter 1. God tells Jonah the same thing in both passages, which is actually pretty sad, because it's a sign of failure on Jonah's part. God had to tell him the same thing twice, because Jonah didn't listen to him the first time. Instead, he bailed out on God so he could avoid that mission.

You would think God would've given up on him after that and looked for someone else to deliver his message to Nineveh. However, it's important to note that God never gave up on Jonah. He kept pursuing Jonah, and he does the same thing to us as well. No matter how many times we ignore him or try to run away from him, he never gives up pursuing us. Despite all our sins and failures, he still loves us as much as ever. He'll keep reaching out to us and won't stop until we finally turn toward him and decide to follow and serve him.

Making that decision to follow him may not always seem easy at the moment; it may take some courage or motivation, but in the long run you'll be glad you chose to listen to God. You'll be amazed at the positive changes God creates in your life or in the life of others or both, and you also may notice that your perspective on life has become more positive than it used to.

This can also serve as a lesson that we shouldn't give up easily on others. This can be tempting at times when people let us down or keep failing us or keep resisting Christ, but remember this: If God is patient enough and loving enough to not give up on us, then we should have that same attitude toward others. He could easily have given up on Jonah or on many others in the Bible—in fact, he could have given up on Israel all together—but he never did, and that persistence paid off. He wants us to emulate that.

Does Jonah try to run away again after hearing God's message a second time? Fortunately, no. Verse 3a says:

> *Jonah obeyed the word of the Lord and went to Nineveh.*

Jonah has learned his lesson and realizes he has to obey God. He can't hide from God, no matter how hard he tries. Any attempt to do so will be disastrous.

Our lives can suffer in the same way when we try to run from God. We're much better off obeying him. Not only can it benefit us to obey God, it can benefit others as well. We'll see a good example of that later in this chapter.

Nineveh

As we noticed earlier, the Bible doesn't tell us much about Nineveh. In fact, the most detailed description about the city comes in verse 3b:

> *Now Nineveh was a very large city; it took three days to go through it.*

That's almost all we learn about it, but it's enough to give us a good idea of what Jonah was walking through. We also learn in 4:11 that Nineveh's population at this time was over 120,000. That may not seem big in this day and age, but back in Jonah's time that was really big for a city.

Nineveh was a thriving city in those days—a hot spot for people to visit and live—but as mentioned earlier, it was a city that didn't believe in God and was cruel toward God's people, the Israelites.

In verse 4, Jonah arrives in Nineveh and finally does what God called him to do at the beginning of the book:

> *Jonah began by going a day's journey into the city, proclaiming, "Forty more days and Nineveh will be overthrown.*

Given what we know about the Ninevites' hatred toward Jonah's people, it wouldn't have been surprising to see them ignore Jonah or do something more harsh: taunt him, assault him, arrest him, or even kill him. Instead, what happens is something unheard of, something unexpected, nothing short of miraculous. Verses 5–9 say:

> *The Ninevites believed God. A fast was proclaimed, and all of them, from the greatest to the least, put on sackcloth. When Jonah's warning reached the king of Nineveh, he rose from his throne, took off his royal robes, covered himself with sackcloth and sat down in the dust. This is the proclamation he issued in Nineveh: "By the decree of the king and his nobles: Do not let people or animals, herds or flocks, taste anything; do not let them eat or drink. But let people and animals be covered with sackcloth. Let*

everyone call urgently on God. Let them give up their
evil ways and their violence. Who knows? God may
yet relent and with compassion turn from his fierce
anger so that we will not perish.'

When you read about people in the Bible covering themselves with sackcloth and dust, it means they were deeply saddened or in a state of mourning. Here we see the Ninevites doing this because not only did they hear Jonah's message, they took it to heart. They realized they had made a huge mistake. They had offended Israel's God, Yahweh, and as a result God was going to punish them by destroying them in 40 days. Even the king of Nineveh took Jonah's message seriously. Not only did he put on sackcloth and sit in dust, he made sure everyone else wore sackcloth as well. He even made sure sackcloth was put on the animals and that no one, human or animal, would eat or drink *anything*. Even more importantly, he also made sure everyone renounced their "evil ways and their violence."

Is this the reaction you would expect to see from a city that doesn't believe in God? Of course not. (Can you imagine one of the countries in today's world that despises Christianity having this kind of reaction to such a message? Probably not. But that was the case with Nineveh). This is the kind of reaction you would expect from people who already believed in God, and even then, some of them might not be completely convinced of the validity of the message. In other words, the very powerful message Jonah delivered affected the entire city of Nineveh to the fullest extent. Everyone humbled themselves before Israel's God, turned their hearts to him, and altered their lives so they could show reverence to him.

The Ninevites are the second group of people Jonah encountered in this book, and each of them came to know God.

Does this mean Jonah was a very gifted speaker?

We don't know how influential Jonah sounded when he delivered this message to Nineveh, but it had to have sounded pretty powerful in order to instantly change the hearts of over 120,000 people whose religious views were completely different than his. In fact, despite the many great speakers and preachers there have been over the centuries, no one has ever come close to converting as many people with a single message as Jonah did. This must mean Jonah's message was the most influential message in human history. Right?

Actually, the reality is that Nineveh's repentance had very little to do with Jonah's speech. It's possible his appearance may have grabbed their attention, because his skin may have been deformed from spending three days and three nights inside the fish, but even that wouldn't have been enough to convince them. The reason they all repented was because the Holy Spirit was at work in their hearts while Jonah was delivering God's message. Keep in mind that Jonah wasn't even trying to convert them. He just told them God was going to kill them all in forty days.

When we talk to people about God and Jesus, they won't take our words seriously unless the Holy Spirit has reached out to them and softened their hearts. People don't seriously choose to put their faith in Christ and start following him on their own. No matter how prepared we are or how skilled we are at speaking, if the Holy Spirit is not at work in their hearts, it doesn't matter how hard we try and how long we speak to them about God and Jesus. They won't believe us or even consider putting their faith in Christ unless the Spirit is at work in their hearts.

When will the Spirit reach out to these people?

Sometimes it can take a while (remember, everything happens on God's timing), and it requires patience and prayer on your part before the Holy Spirit reaches out to another person. However, there are some people he never reaches. It may be sad to think that not everyone is destined for heaven (see Revelation 20:15), but that's the reality of the world we live in.

However, we don't know who is included in the book of life. We have no clue whose hearts are going to be impacted by the Holy Spirit, so we can't assume it'll only happen to certain people and not to others. We also have no clue *when* the Holy Spirit will reach out to people, so we can't ignore any opportunities to talk to people about Christ.

For the Ninevites in the book of Jonah, it was God's will for all of them to be saved after hearing Jonah's message, as you can tell when you read verse 10:

> *When God saw what they did and how they turned from their evil ways, he relented and did not bring on them the destruction he had threatened.*

Wait—didn't God want to destroy Nineveh?

Yes, God was angry with the Ninevites and wanted to bring destruction on them, and Jonah wasn't even trying to convert them when he delivered God's message. But you need to remember that God is also a loving and merciful God who's always willing to give us a second chance. As long as we're alive, there's still a chance for us to repent of our sins and put our faith in Christ. God's like that with everyone (1 Timothy 2:3–4); he doesn't play favorites. It doesn't matter who you are, how you're living your life, or what you've done in the past. What matters is whether or not you're willing to change your life by centering it around God and accepting his son Jesus as your Lord and Savior.

The Israelites in the Old Testament had a misunderstanding about God, and it became more evident in the New Testament; they thought that God only loved *them* and no one else. This isn't true, as we've just discussed, and not only was it a big misunderstanding on their part, that idea also affected the way they viewed and sometimes treated foreigners.

Yes, God once said the Israelites were his chosen people, but the Israelites thought that meant they were the *only* people he loved and wanted a relationship with. What God really meant was that the Israelites were his *servants* who would reach out to the other nations and teach them about him. Unfortunately, the Israelites didn't do that. It wasn't until after Jesus came that they started to understand what they were supposed to do. He made it clear that we need to proclaim the gospel—that he was the son of God, that he came to save us, and that it's only through him that we can be saved—to all nations (Matthew 28:19).

There were some Jews who refused to do that, mainly because they didn't believe Jesus was who he claimed to be. Fortunately, there were some who believed Jesus and obeyed him, including his disciples and the apostle Paul. Those Jews ended up preaching to many foreign nations—also known as Gentile nations—about Jesus and how they can only be saved through Christ. As a result, many countries today believe in Jesus, and those people are spreading the good news to more and more people throughout the world.

Keep in mind that you don't have to be an Israelite to tell others about Jesus. That mission just started with the Israelites. God wants all of us to do that, so more and more people can come to know Jesus and be saved.

That's why God didn't destroy Nineveh. They repented and put their faith in him, and he knew their actions were genuine. It didn't matter that they weren't Israelites; he loved them just as much. Even though Jonah wasn't trying to convert them, God still used him to reach out to this foreign nation that needed his love and forgiveness.

Wait—God had prophesied that Nineveh would be destroyed. Does this mean he had a change of plans when he decided not to destroy Nineveh?

This is a good question. What God told Jonah about destroying Nineveh was a prophecy, and we see God's prophecies come to fruition over and over throughout the many stories in the Bible. However, this time it looks like his prophecy doesn't come true, because he relented from destroying the Ninevites after they humbled themselves before him. The Bible says that God's promises always come to fruition (i.e., 2 Peter 3:9). If he had a change of heart with Nineveh, this could be evidence that his initial plans don't always come to fruition, which can also mean he's flawed—he's emotionally unstable and likely to change his mind with us—and that he can't be fully trusted. Right?

Wrong! Many years after the story of Jonah, the prophet Nahum delivered a message from God to the Ninevites, saying that God was going to destroy them because of how great their sins were … again. This message is recorded in the book of Nahum (another minor prophetic book in the Bible). It's a short book—only three chapters long—and it consists of nothing but bad news for the Ninevites. The first verse of the book even begins with, "A prophecy concerning Nineveh" (Nahum 1:1). In 1:14, God says he'll "destroy" Nineveh's idols, and will "prepare" the Ninevites' "grave" because they're "vile."

Throughout the book of Nahum, God vividly describes how he's in opposition to the Ninevites and will make them suffer because of how sinful they've been. In 3:5–6, God specifically says to Nineveh, "I am against you ... I will lift your skirts over your face. I will show the nations your nakedness and the kingdoms your shame. I will pelt you with filth, I will treat you with contempt and make you a spectacle." In 3:15, he says, "There the fire will consume you; the sword will cut you down—they will devour you like a swarm of locusts." The book ends with God saying, "Nothing can heal you; your wound is fatal. All who hear the news about you clap their hands at your fall, for who has not felt your endless cruelty?" (3:19).

In other words, God is fed up with Nineveh and isn't going to tolerate them any longer. They've turned back to their sinful ways and no longer acknowledge him. Now he's done with the Ninevites and is ready to give them what they deserve.

We see Nineveh mentioned one more time in the Old Testament. It's in the book of Zephaniah (yet another minor prophetic book), and once again the news about Nineveh is not good. The book is only three chapters long, and most of it explains the judgment God is going to bring on various nations. In 2:13, Zephaniah says God will "stretch out his hand against the north and destroy Assyria, leaving Nineveh utterly desolate and dry as the desert."

Unlike the Ninevites in the book of Jonah, the ones referred to in Nahum and Zephaniah have denied God and have made no attempt to repent of their sins and seek God's forgiveness. The generation to which Jonah spoke did a great job of getting their act together, but the later generations reverted to their sinful ways. The time has come for God to fulfill the prophecy that he first had Jonah deliver. The great city of Nineveh will be destroyed soon, and this time God will show no mercy toward them.

In 612 BC, some time after these books were written, God's prophecy came true: the city of Nineveh was destroyed.

What's sad is that the Ninevites had many opportunities to turn back to God, but instead they ignored him and continued to sin and deny God until he became so angry with them that he couldn't tolerate them any longer. The Ninevites basically brought this devastation on themselves. You would think they would've known better, based on what had happened to their ancestors in the book of Jonah, but apparently not.

It's worth noting that God did something similar to his people Israel earlier in the Old Testament. They had been sinful and rebellious toward him for so long, while ignoring his many warnings, that there came a point in which God had had enough of it, so he allowed them to be overrun by their enemy nations. Many Israelites were killed, while others were taken into exile far away from their homeland, which had been devastated. God is definitely a jealous God, and he wants everyone to love him and obey him. When he tells you to do something, he is serious about it.

In other words, God's prophecy of destroying Nineveh did come to fruition. It just came at a much different time than we expected. This is evidence that everything always happens on God's time. We don't always know when something is going to happen, but he does, so we need to trust his timing. He's always in control, he knows what's going to happen in our lives, and he also knows *when* it's going to happen.

Sometimes it can be hard for us to trust God, because we think we know what's supposed to happen in our lives and when it should happen. If it doesn't, then we get confused, worried, and frustrated. We don't just get frustrated at our situation, we also get frustrated with God for messing up our personal plans. It's important to understand that if something doesn't happen, it either means God has a better time for that or has something better planned for us. When something like that happens to us, it can sometimes seem confusing at first, but later, when that event becomes a thing of the past, we'll look back at it and understand why it happened. That's when God's timing will make more sense, and we'll be thankful he allowed the situation to play out like that.

Some people do a good job of staying patient and waiting for God's timing to play out, but others struggle because they want to be in control of the situation. They want to make sure things happen exactly the way they want, and they also want to make sure those things happen at a time they feel is best. The problem is that their plans sometimes conflict with God's, and they have a hard time remembering or accepting the fact that his plans and his timing are better than theirs. If you're one of those who struggle with this control issue, then you need to pray for God to grant you patience, to give you the ability to let go of your attempt to control things and to let God handle it. It's very important you trust God, because he's the only one who knows what's going to happen and when. His plans never fail, and his timing is always right.

Since Nineveh was destroyed later on, does that mean the Ninevites' repentance wasn't genuine?

When you read about Nineveh in the books of Nahum and Zephaniah, it may look like Nineveh's repentance in Jonah was just a sly attempt to prevent God from killing them. But that's not the case at all. No one can cheat God by pretending to repent. God is too smart to fall for that, and he also knows what our hearts are truly like—what we're actually thinking.

This generation of Ninevites to whom Jonah reached out is different than others who came before and after it. It's worth pointing out that Jesus himself talks about these particular Ninevites hundreds of years later—and he doesn't have anything bad to say about them. In Matthew 12:38–41 Jesus is approached by some Pharisees who want him to show them a sign. Jesus responds to them in verses 39–41 by saying:

> *A wicked and adulterous generation asks for a sign! But none will be given it except the sign of the prophet Jonah. For as Jonah was three days and three nights in the belly of a huge fish, so the Son of Man will be three days and three nights in the heart of the earth. The men of Nineveh will stand up at the judgment with this generation and condemn it; for they repented at the preaching of Jonah, and now something greater than Jonah is here* (a similar version of this story is told in Luke 11:29–32).

Keep in mind that these Pharisees were teachers of the Law. It was their job to make sure the Israelites obeyed God's law, and they would punish disobedience accordingly. However, as the years went by, the Pharisees became corrupt and started abusing their power. They made up their own rules and guidelines as to how certain laws were to be obeyed. They became selfish and looked down at everyone else, thinking they were better and that God liked them more than everyone else. When Jesus showed up and started telling everyone he was the son of God and that everyone should follow him, the Pharisees were unconvinced and felt offended by him. Despite the many prophecies Jesus had fulfilled and the miracles he'd performed, the Pharisees didn't believe him, and they hated how he was making them look bad. They tried desperately to find fault in him so they could have a good reason to arrest him.

When this group of Pharisees in Matthew 12:38–41 asked Jesus for a sign, he knew it would be pointless. The hearts of these Pharisees were cold and twisted, and seeing a sign from Jesus wouldn't convince them who he was. Instead, he tells them they'll be condemned for rebuking Jesus and for not believing his messages. To top it off, Jesus says they're going to be judged by the Ninevites, who had repented after hearing Jonah's message.

On one hand, you have the Ninevites, who didn't believe in God and yet repented after hearing a message from someone much lesser than Jesus. On the other hand, you have the Pharisees, who believed in God and knew the scriptures really well—and they were supposed to be much better people than the Ninevites—and yet most of them didn't repent after hearing many great messages and witnessing some amazing miracles from Jesus himself. This isn't what you would expect to happen at all.

It's kind of funny how we see these ironic twists play out between the Pharisees during Jesus's time and Jonah in the book of Jonah. Jonah was supposed to be the best example for us to follow in that story, but instead he's the only bad example. Likewise, the Pharisees were supposed to be great examples for us to follow in the New Testament, but instead they're the worst examples. The good examples in all these stories are not the people you expect: the sailors, the Ninevites, the peasants, the fishermen, the sick and the lame, etc. God is obviously trying to make a point in these stories—that you can't assume some people are better than others. We're all equally important. We all can be saved, and it doesn't matter what your life is currently like or what you've done in the past. God loves all of us, and he doesn't play favorites. He's waiting for each of us to turn to him, confess our sins, and put our faith in Christ. He'll lovingly welcome everyone who does that.

Also, God doesn't want us to be selfish or to look down on anyone—what Jesus accused the Pharisees of doing. Instead, he wants us to humble ourselves, as the Ninevites did, and view everyone as equal. That mindset evokes the fruits of the Holy Spirit (Galatians 5:22–23), including peace, love, and kindness—all of which are biblical traits that God loves to see in us.

In other words, what Jesus was hinting at is that the Ninevites from Jonah's time are actually *better* examples than the Pharisees from his time. The Ninevites showed us how we're supposed to respond to God, while the Pharisees showed us how *not* to respond to God. When the Ninevites heard Jonah's message, they humbled themselves before God and sought forgiveness. When the Pharisees heard Jesus's message, they practically spat in his face. They were more interested in their own image. They wanted to look perfect, mighty, smart, and more powerful than everyone else. But God doesn't want us to act like that at all. He wants us to humble ourselves and be more like the Ninevites in the book of Jonah.

That's actually how *Jesus* lived his life on Earth—he didn't just humble himself before God, he also humbled himself before others. In Philippians 2:5–8, the apostle Paul clarifies Jesus's mindset and explains how we need to be the same way. He says:

> *In your relationships with one another, have the same mindset as Christ Jesus: Who, being in very nature God, did not consider equality with God something to be used to his own advantage; rather, he made himself nothing by taking the very nature of a servant, being made in human likeness. And being found in appearance as a man, he humbled himself by being obedient to death—even death on a cross!*

That's the mindset the Ninevites adopted in Jonah 3. Not only did it please God, we learn from Jesus centuries later that those Ninevites are in heaven. The group of Pharisees that spoke to Jesus in Matthew 12:38–41 were not bound for heaven, because their hearts were cold—they were so selfish, legalistic, and deceiving that they didn't truly love God, and they also rejected Jesus and his teachings. They had the absolute wrong mindset for being a follower of God. In fact, it's the complete opposite of what Philippians 2:5–8 says. What that passage describes is more of the mindset that the Ninevites adopted. In other words, the Ninevites in Jonah are much better examples for us to follow than the Pharisees during Jesus's time (which is pretty sad, because the Pharisees were supposed to be great examples for God's people to follow).

So that's how chapter 3 ends. You would think this would be a great place to end the book of Jonah. Jonah has obeyed God and delivered his message; the people of Nineveh have heard it, and have all turned their hearts to God, seeking forgiveness; and God has relented from his anger, deciding not to destroy Nineveh. And they all lived happily ever after. Right?

Unfortunately, that's not the case. There's still a big issue in this story that needs to be resolved. It doesn't have anything to do with Nineveh, though (if anything, they're the ones who lived happily ever after). It has to do with the one person in this story you wouldn't expect to still be dealing with issues, and that's Jonah. He seemed to have learned his lesson and to be on good terms with God. But there's a big issue he's still dealing with, and God is about to confront him about it. That's the purpose of chapter 4—unveiling and at least attempting to resolve Jonah's issue.

CHAPTER 4

JONAH AND GOD

IT'S TIME NOW to dive into the last chapter of Jonah. One could view this as an epilogue to the story, especially if you think the main purpose of this book is to show how Nineveh was saved from condemnation. However, it may be more accurate to view this chapter as the denouement—the conclusion of the story. The main purpose of this book is to get Jonah to obey God and to also learn a very important lesson from God. God communicates that lesson to him in chapter 4.

We learn all too well in this chapter that Jonah's mindset is not on the same page as God's. In fact, they seem to be polar opposites. This may sound surprising, because Jonah is a prophet of God, and it seemed as though he learned from his mistakes earlier in this book. He learned he can't run from God and is much better off obeying him. In fact, in chapter 2 Jonah prayed as if he were eager to do that, and in chapter 3 he immediately obeyed God when God told him to go to Nineveh and deliver his message.

You would think Jonah would've been excited to see the Ninevites repent and to also see God have mercy on them. Unfortunately, we learn in chapter 4 that that's not the case at all. His reaction is the complete opposite of what you'd expect from one of God's people. Verse 1 says:

> *But to Jonah this seemed very wrong, and he became angry.*

If that reaction seems kind of confusing to you, that is understandable. Jonah apparently had bitter feelings toward Nineveh, and he had been hiding it all this time. He didn't think Nineveh deserved to be saved, and now his frustration is starting to show.

A lot of people can be angry like this and hide it from others. Something good will happen to someone, a legitimate cause for celebration, but someone else will be disappointed in the outcome and won't want to celebrate or even congratulate that person. Sometimes this is simply because their heart is filled with greed or selfishness; other times it's because they have bitter feelings toward that person, which is the case with Jonah toward the Ninevites.

To top it off, a person will sometimes keep those bitter feelings to themselves, so no one knows about it. They'll pretend everything is okay and make no attempt to address the issue. The problem is that this issue affects their heart, and it won't get better over time—if anything, it'll only get worse—unless they try to fix it. Some people think they can simply ignore that bitter feeling, but that doesn't make it go away. It'll still be there simmering within you, and as time goes by it will start to affect your image and your relationships in negative ways. Eventually those feelings will burst out of you in a real ugly way, and this dark side of you will be exposed to everyone, including people from whom you were trying to hide these feelings.

Even if you feel like you have succeeded in hiding your feelings, there's still one person from whom you can never hide them, and that's God. He's well aware of what you're thinking, and he'll see the displeasure in your heart the moment it forms—there's no point in trying to hide it from him. You need to go to him about the issue and work on resolving it. If you continue to struggle with it, then you need to seek help. Some people don't feel comfortable doing that, which is understandable, but there are no good excuses for putting aside an issue like this. You still need to push yourself to get it resolved. The sooner you work on it, the better, both for you and the people in your life.

We just learned that Jonah was angry about what happened to Nineveh. However, there was something else bothering him that he had talked to God about earlier, but we don't learn about it until here in verses 2–3 (and it's really interesting):

> He prayed to the Lord, "Isn't this what I said, Lord, when I was still at home? That is what I tried to forestall by fleeing to Tarshish. I knew that you are a gracious and compassionate God, slow to anger and abounding in love, a God who relents from sending calamity. Now, Lord, take away my life, for it is better for me to die than to live."

So Jonah knew from the beginning that this was going to happen to Nineveh! And yet he didn't *want* it to happen! He knew that if he obeyed God that the Ninevites would be saved, but he didn't *want* them to be saved! That's not at all the attitude God wants us to have toward others, and you definitely wouldn't expect one of God's prophets to have that kind of mindset. If we love everyone, which is what God wants us to do, we'll want all of them to be saved, *regardless* of who they are.

It seemed as though Jonah had a change of heart back in chapter 2, but you need to remember that he was probably terrified and convinced he was about to die. It's possible that in the back of his mind he still didn't want to go to Nineveh, but he knew he had no other choice. He had to obey God, and he was willing to do that so he could stay alive and not make God angry in a way that would cause him to wreak havoc with Jonah again.

This would imply that Jonah was serving God reluctantly when he went to Nineveh, which isn't at all the attitude God wants us to have when serving him. However, it's possible that Jonah went to Nineveh thinking that maybe, just maybe, the Ninevites might not repent and God would actually destroy them. Apparently, Jonah was so bitter toward the Ninevites that he would have loved to see that happen. Even though the odds of that happening were next to none, he still may have been motivated to go to Nineveh in case such a thing actually happened to the Ninevites.

Why does Jonah want to die?

Jonah is obviously very upset at God's showing mercy toward Nineveh, and now he's overreacting.

Unfortunately, this isn't the first time we see one of God's prophets talking like this. In 1 Kings 19:4 we see Elijah asking God to also take his life. In some ways this is even more surprising, because Elijah seems like a much more obedient and God-fearing prophet than Jonah. But in 1 Kings 19:4 he has an unexpected slip up.

Elijah had just defeated 450 prophets of Baal (a popular false god in those days) in a competition to prove which god was more powerful—Baal or Elijah's God Yahweh. Making a long story short, Baal didn't do anything when his prophets called on him to act, but God acted the moment Elijah called on him. God did so in an amazing way that made it clear not only that he actually existed, but also that he was more powerful than Baal. Elijah was confident from the beginning he would win the competition, and afterward he had all those prophets of Baal killed.

This was a big loss for king Ahab, who witnessed it all. When he went home and told his wife, Jezebel, about it, she sent a message to Elijah saying she was going to kill him.

You wouldn't think this would bother Elijah, especially since he knows God is on his side, and he knows how powerful God is (he also just got a glimpse of it during the competition). Instead, he panics. According to 1 Kings 19:4a, Elijah ends up traveling "a day's journey into the wilderness." That's not the reaction you'd expect from him. To top it off, verse 4b says, "He came to a broom bush, sat down under it and prayed that he might die. 'I have had enough, Lord,' he said. 'Take my life; I am no better than my ancestors.'"

God didn't kill Elijah. He knew that Elijah's human fallibility was affecting him during that moment. He just needed to be taught, or possibly be reminded of, an important lesson. In Jonah 4:3 God sees it happening to another one of his prophets—this time it's Jonah. As with his treatment of Elijah, God didn't kill him. Instead, he used the opportunity to teach Jonah an important lesson.

These are great examples showing that no matter how strong our faith is in God and no matter how knowledgeable we are of God and the Bible, we still have moments where we stumble and fall short of his glory (see Romans 3:23).

None of us is perfect. No matter how close we are to God, at some point we're going to stumble in our walk with him. Unfortunately, there are a lot of ways in which we can stumble: we give in to temptation and commit a sin, we choose to ignore

God's calling, we doubt he'll answer our prayers, we think we're not good enough for God, etc.

Although God is at work in our lives and is building us up to be more like Christ, the problem is that he's not the only one at work in our lives. The enemy, Satan, is desperately working hard to pull us away from God. He's the one who plants seeds of temptation and doubt in our minds. He's the one who makes us think we're not good enough for God, that God doesn't love us or forgive us, that God can't provide for us, or that there are better things out there than God. None of that is true!

We need to ignore those negative thoughts and resist the temptations Satan brings into our lives. We can do that by standing firm in God's light and staying focused on his love and compassion, which he generously offers *all* of us. No matter how hard Satan tries to pull us down, God is *always* there to help us fight back. He'll never leave us for any reason (Deuteronomy 31:8), and we need to be willing to call on him for help whenever we feel like Satan is trying pull us down.

It's also important to point out that God understands how Jonah is feeling right now. In fact, God knows how *each* of us is feeling *all* the time. He knows when we're happy, and he wants to rejoice with us. He knows when we're angry, sad, or anxious, and he wants to comfort us. However, if we want him to help us get over those negative feelings, we need to ask him for help and we need to trust him to get the job done.

Jonah's heart isn't in the right place at this moment, and God is well aware of that. In verse 4, his response to Jonah is short and simple:

> But the Lord replied, 'Is it right for you to be angry?'

We don't know what Jonah's response was to that question or if he even gave a response. If anything else was said between them during this moment, it wasn't documented in this book. Regardless, God just made his point clear to Jonah: Jonah has no right to be angry with God's actions. God treats Nineveh the same way he treats Israel and everyone else; he shows mercy to *all* who love him, seek him, and repent of their sins.

Has Jonah learned his lesson yet?

There seems to be a gap of time between verses 4 and 5. When you read verse 5, it sounds like the conversation we just saw between God and Jonah has been over for a while, and Jonah has moved on. Now it's time to see if Jonah has learned his lesson. We find out in a very interesting way in verses 5-9:

> *Jonah had gone out and sat down at a place east of the city. There he made himself a shelter, sat in its shade and waited to see what would happen to the city. Then the Lord God provided a leafy plant and made it grow up over Jonah to give shade for his head to ease his discomfort, and Jonah was very happy about the plant. But at dawn the next day God provided a worm, which chewed the plant so that it withered. When the sun rose, God provided a scorching east wind, and the sun blazed on Jonah's head so that he grew faint. He wanted to die, and said, 'It would be better for me to die than to live.'*
>
> *But God said to Jonah, 'Is it right for you to be angry about the plant?'*
>
> *"It is," he said. "And I'm so angry I wish I were dead.'*

Once again, Jonah becomes so upset he overreacts and wishes he were dead. It doesn't appear he's learned his lesson yet.

Notice how God handled this. Jonah is looking to see if God will destroy Nineveh, but God has no intention of doing that. He could have simply told Jonah, "I'm not going to destroy it." Instead, he provides Jonah with shade while he waits and watches to see if Nineveh will be destroyed. It seems that God is being generous, but then he sends a worm to eat the plant so that Jonah suddenly no longer has any shade. Then he makes Jonah so hot and miserable that he once again wishes he were dead. Does this make sense? Why would God do this?

It's probably safe to assume that God has a sense of humor, but right now he's not joking around. He was using that plant as a metaphor to help make an important point, but Jonah was completely oblivious to it. In verses 10–11 (the last two verses of the book), God makes that point clear to him:

> But the Lord said, 'You have been concerned about this plant, though you did not tend it or make it grow. It sprang up overnight and died overnight. And should I not have concern for the great city of Nineveh, in which there are more than a hundred and twenty thousand people who cannot tell their right hand from their left—and also many animals?'

And that is how the book of Jonah ends. It isn't the happy ending you would expect, especially given how chapter 3 ended. If anything, it probably seems anti-climactic, incomplete, and probably also confusing.

Remember, this isn't a fairy tale where you have a clear-cut beginning and ending, with character development, a big climax, and a happy ending. This is a story about Jonah that was written for the purpose of teaching us about God and how we should live our lives.

These last two verses can seem a little confusing, though, especially if you don't read it, as well as the rest of this chapter, very carefully. Let's start with what God said about the Ninevites not knowing their right hand from their left hand. You may be wondering if he meant that literally or if it was a figure of speech. It's safe to assume the Ninevites—or at least most of them—were educated enough to know the difference between their right and left hands. This is likely a metaphorical way of saying the Ninevites didn't know the difference between right and wrong. After all, they had never known God and instead had false gods that they had believed in and worshipped for many generations. They were very misled and were living sinful lives without realizing it, but God still cared for them and wanted them to love him and put their faith in him. He had every right to be concerned for these lost people.

What might confuse people the most about this book is that it ends with God asking Jonah a question—and it doesn't get answered. In fact, we don't even get a response from Jonah. There are only two books in the Bible that end with a question, and this is one of them. The other is Nahum (call it a coincidence, if you want, that Nineveh shows up in both books).

It might seem kind of strange to end the story like this. However, if you read those last two verses carefully, you'll realize it's a rhetorical question, and it's pretty obvious what the answer is: God *should* be concerned about the people of Nineveh.

Also, God points out in these last two verses that Jonah was concerned about the plant, and yet he did nothing to help it. As a result, the plant died. Likewise, God was concerned about the people of Nineveh, who are obviously a lot more important than a plant. If nothing had been done to help them, they all would have died, just like that plant. Instead, God took action and used Jonah to save the Ninevites from death, both physically and spiritually.

We need to be willing to do the same to those who don't know Christ. If no attempt is made to reach out to them, they're going to grow up, die, and spend all eternity separated from God and his love, glory, and mercy. That's why it's so important we look for opportunities to reach out to others. You don't always know when that opportunity is going to come up, but when it does, you need to be ready to act. You can end up being responsible for leading someone to Christ. You might only have one opportunity to reach out to that person, so you need to be prepared for that moment.

Unfortunately, Jonah had no love or concern for the Ninevites whatsoever. That's an attitude we should never have toward anyone, regardless of who they are and what they've done. Remember, God commands us to love everyone. Unfortunately, Jonah seemed to have forgotten about that. (If he didn't forget about it, then he definitely had a hard time following that commandment.)

In fact, it's also important to point out that Jonah was more concerned about a *plant* than the lives of over 120,000 people. Does that make sense? Of course not. Once again, this isn't at all the mindset you would expect to see from one of God's prophets.

The plant

It's kind of sad how the only thing that mattered to Jonah toward the end of this story was a plant. He was more interested in that than all the people of Nineveh whom God loved and wanted to save. God was very concerned about Nineveh, but Jonah was too selfish and stubborn to realize that, even after God had spoken to him in 4:4. Instead he became interested in a significantly less important plant.

That plant ended up being a distraction to Jonah because it turned his attention away from much more important things on which God wanted him to focus. He should've been alarmed and concerned about the Ninevites, but instead his feelings toward them were cold and unforgiving. He wanted to watch them die while sitting comfortably in the shade next to his pretty little plant.

We may not all be interested in plants, but figuratively speaking we each have our own "plant" that distracts us and turns our minds away from more important things in life on which God wants us to be focused. For some people, their plant is video games: they're more interested in playing video games than they are in helping God's people. For others their plant is sports: they're more interested in playing and/or watching sports than they are in serving God. For others, their plant is social media: they're more interested in spending time on social media than they are in spending time in the Bible. Plants can come in many other forms, including TV, music, books, working out, eating, drinking, gambling, porn, fishing, hunting, art, and any other number of hobbies, activities, and addictions that can distract your heart. Even your job can be a plant.

Most of the activities listed are not inherently sinful. It's okay to do most of them, but you can't let them consume your life so much that you become more concerned about them than about more significant things in life on which God wants you to be focused. He wants us to be focused on our relationships with him and others, and he also wants us to serve him to help accomplish his will. We can't do any of that if we're distracted by "plants."

There could be people in your life to whom God wants you to reach out, or he might want you to serve him in a specific way. But you either haven't noticed it yet, or you've noticed it and aren't interested because you're too comfortable and occupied with a "plant" in your life. It's very important you either turn away from it or spend less time with it (depending on what that plant is) because you could easily be missing out on opportunities to serve God and reach out to those who need Jesus in their life.

Also, if you make no attempt to turn your focus away from that plant, God will send a "worm" to disrupt your plant like he did with Jonah. You probably won't like it when that happens (you may have noticed that Jonah was furious when God did it to him), but it'll be a wakeup call that God wants you to change your mindset and possibly also your lifestyle.

It's really important you take a moment to look at your life and see if there are any "plants" that are distracting you from God and his people. Not only can they distract you but they can also make you selfish, concerned only about yourself. (Jonah became so selfish he wanted to die right then and there after he'd lost his plant.) God doesn't want us to act like that at all.

Jonah made the mistake of letting an insignificant plant consume his life; don't make the same mistake by getting consumed with your own "plant." That's not what God is calling you to do. Focusing too much on a plant will get you nowhere in your spiritual journey. It can make God upset (and you definitely don't want to do that), and it can also mess up your life or the lives of others or both. The Bible has many examples of people making God upset with their poor decisions, and then God making them pay the price in a big way. Sometimes their poor decisions only hurt just them; other times it hurts others whom they didn't want to suffer. It was all part of the consequence of their poor decisions.

In other words, don't get distracted from the big picture in life—loving and serving God, and loving and helping others. That should *always* be your focus, not on plants. Plants are ultimately meaningless. (The writer of Ecclesiastes would call them "a chasing after the wind," because they're meaningless, they don't fully satisfy us, and they don't gain us anything in God's eyes.) That's the point God made to Jonah in the last two verses of the book.

What was Jonah's response to God's question after verse 11?

Unfortunately, we don't know how Jonah responded, because it's not documented in the story. It's possible he didn't say anything because he understood the point God had just made or because he needed some time to think about what God had just said. However, in 4:2 you may have noticed that Jonah referenced a conversation he had had earlier with God that was not documented in this story. He said, "Isn't this what I said, Lord, when I was still at home?" The conversation he's referencing would've happened toward the beginning of chapter 1, but the writer did not include it. This could mean there were other conversations between God and Jonah that the writer decided not to include (most likely he felt they weren't necessary or even relevant to the story). If that's the case, then it's very possible that 4:11 was not the end of God's and Jonah's conversation.

Given that Jonah was a prophet who spoke with God and knew the scriptures really well, it's safe to assume he understood the point God made in those last two verses. The real question is: did he take that lesson to heart, or was he too stubborn to accept it and still upset at God for not destroying Nineveh?

All we can do is imagine Jonah's response, if he had one. Just don't spend too much time thinking about it, because that's not the point of this story. The Bible already has some books that have unintentionally caused Christians to debate insignificant topics. For example, there are some who debate the authorship of the book of Hebrews. It's the only book in the New Testament in which the author is unknown, but trying to figure out who wrote it is not why Hebrews was written. Likewise, the book of Jonah was not written so people could debate what happened after 4:11. We can wonder about it a little, but we needn't get caught up in pointless topics such as that with Jonah or any other book in the Bible. We should be focused on the many important things that *were* written in Jonah as well as in the other books in the Bible.

Why would the writer end the story like that?

Unfortunately, we have no way of knowing. It's possible the writer of this story felt there was nothing else worth writing about, because the biggest lesson in the book had just been clarified and all the events in the story were already complete (the ship battling the storm, Jonah trapped in the fish, Nineveh being saved, and the worm eating the plant). We may just have to wait until we get to heaven some day and ask God, or maybe even ask Jonah himself, what his response was to God's last remark in the book. For now, it's best not to worry about it. If it had been important for us to know about then the writer would have included it in the book. Remember, all scripture is "God-breathed," meaning the Holy Spirit helped these writers write the books of the Bible, including Jonah. This book has told us everything God wants us to know.

And you may have noticed it tells us a lot of important things that we *all* need to know.

Other Thoughts on the Book of Jonah

Why is Jonah such a bad prophet?

It's kind of hard to tell, especially since Jonah seemed like a good prophet in 2 Kings 14:25. One can't help but wonder if God hardened his heart as he did with Pharaoh in the book of Exodus. In that story, there are multiple instances in which Moses is trying to convince Pharaoh to let the Israelites leave Egypt, but God kept hardening Pharaoh's heart so that he wouldn't let them go.

As a result, Moses ended up performing many miraculous signs via the power of God while trying to convince Pharaoh to let the Israelites go. If God had not hardened Pharaoh's heart, there would have been no need for God to perform all these amazing miracles, which means we would never have seen his awesome power on display.

In the book of Jonah, it's possible that God hardened Jonah's heart so that Jonah would disobey him. As a result, God had to use his power to bring Jonah back to the mainland via a vicious storm and a fish, and then he used his Holy Spirit to reach out to the hearts of over 120,000 people when Jonah wasn't even trying to convert them. After that he created the plant that stubborn Jonah used for shade, and then sent a worm to eat the plant to help teach Jonah an important lesson that he really needed to know about.

Keep in mind that this is just a possibility. The book doesn't actually say God hardened Jonah's heart like he did Pharaoh's (it might seem like it because of the way Jonah acts throughout the story, but we don't know that for a fact). The reason Jonah may seem like a bad prophet could simply be because, like everyone else, Jonah is not perfect. One of his biggest flaws is exposed in this story. Or maybe we just saw him during a low moment of his career, and he got careless and allowed his sinful nature to get the better of him. Whatever the reason is, it led to him making some huge mistakes that were magnified a lot more than that of any other prophet in the Bible. This is sad, because it didn't seem like he had made any mistakes earlier in 2 Kings 14:25, when God had him deliver an important message to Jeroboam.

It may not seem fair to have Jonah's flaws on display like this. (How would you like it if someone wrote a popular book about a bunch of mistakes you made in a particular situation, and it was read and studied by many people for centuries?) But it's actually beneficial for us to be aware of these flaws. They can help us to better understand things like how *not* to live our lives, how we *should* live our lives, how loving and merciful and powerful God is, how it's not possible for us to run from God, and so on.

It also gives us assurance that Jonah is human like the rest of us. No one is free of sinning or making mistakes, no matter how close they seem to God. This includes prophets, pastors, and Biblical theologians. We're all the same. We all make mistakes, we all sin, and we all fall short of God's glory from time to time.

Good examples, bad examples

As you may have noticed, the book of Jonah gives us some great examples of how we should and should not live our lives. What's ironic about these examples is who they come from. Apart from God, the characters in this book are a prophet who believes in God, a group of sailors who don't believe in God, and the people of a city who also don't believe in God. From that description, you would assume that the prophet is the only character in the book who serves as a good example of how we should live our lives. But that isn't true at all. In fact, he's the *only* bad example in the whole story. We see all these great examples of how we should live our lives—how we should gladly obey God, love him, praise him, and humble ourselves before him—and none of those examples comes from the prophet Jonah. (Yes, Jonah eventually obeyed God, and he had a good prayer in chapter 2; but he tried really hard to avoid God's calling, and when he did obey God he did so reluctantly). These good examples all come from the characters who *don't* believe in God – the sailors and the Ninevites. Meanwhile, the bad examples all come from one person, and it's the *only* person in the story who believes in God—Jonah.

Sometimes you have to expect the unexpected with God. He works in mysterious ways throughout the Bible, but he does it to teach us some valuable lessons—some of which can cause us to radically change our line of thinking. Here he's trying to teach us that people like Jonah are flawed like everyone else. We can't assume that some Christians are better than others or that some Christians aren't very close to God. We also can't assume that some people are destined to be saved or that some are not. It's unfair and can also be inaccurate to make assumptions. As we talked about earlier, God loves everyone and wants us to view others as equals.

Does this mean we shouldn't look up to or trust people like pastors or the prophets in Bible? Not at all! They need to be respected, trusted, and supported. Also, pastors are supposed to teach us about Christ, the Bible, and how we should live our lives. It's important that we respect them and listen to their teachings. If you see evidence that a specific pastor is teaching something heretical, *that's* when you know you can't trust them and are better off keeping your distance from them. If you feel confident enough, you can even try calling them out on their teachings so they can stop misleading people.

How is it possible that the non-believers in Jonah are good examples while the one believer is a bad example?

The reason is quite simple: God reached out to the non-believers—the sailors and the Ninevites—and changed their hearts so they could love him and worship him. Even though Jonah believed in God, he was selfish and wanted God's love to be just for him and his people, the Israelites. This is a big flaw of Jonah's that God pointed out to him in chapter 4. He doesn't want anyone to be selfish (Philippians 2:3).

Jonah vs. Jesus

This may surprise some people, but you can make a lot of interesting comparisons and contrasts between Jonah and Jesus. We mentioned earlier that they both have a story of being in a deep sleep on a boat during a vicious storm, in which all others on the boat were fearing for their lives, and they had to be awakened to help. However, that only scratches the surface of links between these two.

First of all, both men loved God. However, Jonah only wanted himself and the Israelites to experience God's love, while Jesus wanted *everyone* on earth to experience God's love. Jonah embarked on his mission reluctantly, while Jesus gladly embarked on his missions. Jonah was selfish and tried to hide from God, while Jesus was unselfish and always stayed close to God.

From those comparisons alone, you would naturally assume that Jesus's missions in the four Gospels were huge successes while Jonah's mission in the book of Jonah was an utter failure. Surprisingly, that's not the case at all. Here's where the comparisons between the two get really interesting: Jonah preached a message of doom and destruction, and his audience took it to heart, humbled themselves before God, repented, and were saved as a result. Jonah didn't even *try* to make them repent and didn't *want* them to repent either, yet they did it anyway. Meanwhile, Jesus preached a lot of messages of salvation and encouraged people to put their faith in him, but most of his audience didn't believe him. He *wanted* everyone to be saved, but instead they scolded him for what he said and eventually killed him as a result.

Fortunately, there were a few who believed what Jesus said, and they were the ones who ended up spreading the gospel. However, most people hated Jesus for what he was saying and doing, and they kept trying to get him arrested. As for Jonah, no one had any grudge against him whatsoever, and no attempt was made to harm him or arrest him for what he did. (Yes, the sailors threw him overboard in chapter 1, but they weren't trying to harm him; they were only doing what Jonah told them to do, and even then were very reluctant to do that.)

Finally, here's a symbolic comparison between Jonah and Jesus: Jonah was swallowed by a fish in the depths of the sea, and he was there for three days and three nights before God delivered him back out to land, alive and well. Jesus, meanwhile, was killed and buried in a tomb, and he was there for three days and three nights before God brought him back to life and delivered him out of the tomb, alive and well. Jesus even alludes to this symbolic connection between him and Jonah, in Matthew 12:40, while talking to a group of Pharisees (we mentioned this passage earlier when we talked about how Jesus condemned those Pharisees and said they would be judged by the Ninevites). This conversation took place before his death and resurrection, so Jesus was prophesying what was going to happen to him.

Why would more people listen to Jonah than Jesus?

The answer is quite simple: God was at work in the hearts of the Ninevites who heard Jonah, but he had hardened the hearts of the Pharisees who heard Jesus. We can tell from reading the four Gospels that Jesus was a great speaker, but it's important to remember that when you're trying to reach out to someone, it doesn't matter how skilled you are at communicating. If the Holy Spirit is at work in their hearts, as he was with the Ninevites, they'll listen and take you seriously. If the Holy Spirit *isn't* at work in their hearts, as he wasn't with the Pharisees, they won't listen or take you seriously, even if you spend a lot of time and effort reaching out to them.

The Pharisees saw Jesus perform many great miracles, yet most of them were unconvinced he was who he claimed to be—the Son of God. That may seem surprising, maybe even hard to believe, but that's how hard their hearts were. They didn't believe Jesus, even though the evidence was clearly right there in front of them.

If someone as flawed as Jonah is capable of getting hundreds of thousands of people to put their faith in God, surely we, with our own flaws and imperfections, are capable of getting at least one person to believe in God. When you start working with someone, they won't always get converted immediately. Sometimes it'll take a while, so don't give up on that person if they don't believe you at first. Be patient with them, and remember to pray for the Holy Spirit to be at work in their heart. If it becomes obvious after a while that that person isn't going to believe you, then it might be okay to stop working with them and start looking for someone else to try saving.

This is where it helps to have good discernment, which is one of the gifts of the Holy Spirit that you can obtain through prayer and practice. You can use discernment to help find people you feel have the potential to be saved. If they don't listen to you at first, you can use discernment to figure out whether it's worth continuing to pursue them. You don't want to give up too soon on someone, but at the same time you don't want to spend too much time reaching out to someone when it obvious they're not interested and don't believe you.

If you reach a point at which you have to give up trying to save someone, especially after trying really hard, don't think it's your fault. Chances are you didn't do anything wrong. The reason that person didn't get converted is simply because the Holy Spirit is not at work in their heart. People will only want to be saved if the Holy Spirit is at work in their heart.

Remember that not everyone is destined to be saved. If you're unable to convert someone, it's either because their name isn't in the book of life or because God's will is for them to be saved later in life, either by you or by someone else.

Mistakes to avoid when evangelizing

What's tricky about reaching out to others about Jesus—also known as evangelizing—is that you have no way of knowing beforehand who will believe you and who won't believe you. A big mistake you can make is to assume a certain person will listen and a certain person won't. You need to be brave and willing to reach out and evangelize to everyone with the open idea that anyone can be saved. You may be surprised at who listens to you and who doesn't. For example, in the story of Jonah, you would never have guessed that the sailors and the Ninevites would take God seriously and be saved. In the four Gospels, you would never have guessed that the Pharisees would rebuke our Lord and Savior, Jesus Christ, especially after seeing him give many great speeches and perform amazing miracles that no one else was capable of doing. If you don't reach out to someone simply because you assume they're not going to be saved, then you're not giving that person an opportunity to be saved.

Jesus doesn't want us to sit idly like that and not try to reach out to people about him. He wants us to preach the gospel to the whole world (Mark 16:15). We shouldn't be afraid to speak to others about Christ. Everyone needs to be given an opportunity to experience God's love and mercy. They can only experience it if they put their faith in Christ. But if no one tells them how to do that, they're likely not going to get saved, because they won't know how.

Unfortunately, when Jonah delivered his message to the Ninevites, he wasn't interested in saving them. He just wanted his enemies to be killed, because he was so biased against them, which is an attitude we should never have toward anyone. Remember,

God loves everyone, and he wants everyone to love each other and to also love him back. There may be people in your life you don't like for various reasons, but the reality is that you may be the only one who has an opportunity to reach out to them. If you summon up the courage to reach out to them, they could get saved because of you. Not only will their lives be transformed, but you'll also have a much better relationship with them—a relationship you probably didn't think was possible. If you've ever wronged them in the past, they'll be willing to forgive you. If they've ever wronged you in the past, you should definitely be willing to forgive them, even before you reach out to them.

In fact, if you're unable to save them, you should *still* be willing to forgive them. After all, God is willing to forgive us for all our many and terrible sins, so we should be willing to forgive others regardless of who they are or what they've done (Matthew 6:14–15 and Colossians 3:13).

Another mistake you can make is to become distracted by plants, like what happened to Jonah in chapter 4, which we talked about earlier. Not only can plants distract us from God, but they can also distract us from the opportunities we have to evangelize to others. If you're more interested or concerned about a plant than on reaching out to someone who doesn't know Jesus, then you need to change your mindset and maybe also ask God for guidance or motivation. You may even have to give up on that plant altogether. It may not be an easy decision at first, but in the long run you'll definitely be glad you chose to pursue God and not that plant. You'll be rewarded spiritually and will also obtain a much deeper satisfaction with your life.

When Jonah was in Nineveh, his heart should've been focused on the Ninevites; instead, it was focused on a plant. In Jonah 4:11 God implied that he was a lot more concerned about Nineveh than the plant, and he's also like that with regard to our lives as well as the lives of those around us. If God is concerned about people like the Ninevites living in sin, then we should be concerned about the people in the world right now that we know are living in sin. Those are the people God is concerned for right now, not a plant. He knows they need to be saved, and he also knows we have the potential to reach out to them.

We can't just sit back and wait for them to die, knowing they'll be condemned for all eternity. That's not loving at all. We need to be as concerned for them as God is. We should want to see them put their faith in Christ. We need to be praying for the Holy Spirit to be at work in them. We need to be on the lookout for opportunities to reach out to them. We need to love them as God loves us, while hoping they get saved at some point, either through us or though someone else if they turn their backs on us. That's the mindset God wants us to have toward them. Nothing else should matter.

Even if you're not able to convert many people, that's okay. Luke 15:7 says that heaven rejoices every time someone is saved! That doesn't mean you can stop trying after you've converted one person. What matters is whether or not you're trying to reach out to others out of love to help God's kingdom grow. That is what God wants us to do. If he was once concerned about the Ninevites living in sin, then he surely is concerned about everyone today who's living in sin. We should be concerned about all of those people, too. That's the mindset God wants us to have, and we see some great examples of that throughout the Bible, with Jesus being arguably the best example for us to follow.

Jonah, however, served as a bad example. He looked down on others and was more concerned about a plant than about people who were lost and needed to be saved. That's the complete opposite of the mindset God wants us to have. He wants us to be very concerned for others and to humble ourselves before others regardless of who they are.

Jonah should've been a great example of how we should live our lives, but he failed miserably in this story. Let's not make the same mistakes he made. Instead, let's serve as good examples to others of how they should live their lives and teach them about Christ. That's what God wants us to do, and the end result can be even better than we can imagine.

You'd be surprised at the amazing things God can do through you if you put your trust in him and obey him. Remember that you can do all things through Christ, who gives you strength (Philippians 4:13).

So many Bible references in this short book

Lastly, you may have noticed that a lot of passages throughout the Bible were referenced while explaining the book of Jonah, both its story lessons and its lessons. It's pretty amazing how easy it is to make so many different connections between Jonah and the other books in the Bible, both the ones written before it and the ones written after it. You can almost think of this book as being a crossroad in the Bible because of that, which makes it even more symbolic that it's located near the middle of the Bible. Not only is this evidence that Jonah is the word of God, it's also evidence that Jonah can be trusted, because the other books in the Bible support its teachings.

That's how important this book is in the Bible. We need to pay attention to it and take it seriously. Not only are there a lot of important lessons in it, it's also intertwined with the other books in the Bible.

Also, knowing about the connections that can be made between Jonah and the other books in the Bible may encourage you to also read and study those other books. You can easily learn some knew and important things from them just like you did with Jonah. After all, they're all God's Word, and God wants us to be familiar with *all* of them. They each have their own lessons and stories that are important for us to know. Jonah is just one of sixty-six that we need to learn about, but as you may have noticed by now, it stands out from the majority of them because of its uniqueness. It truly is an interesting book, being so short and yet still having a lot of details in the story, including some bizarre and unexpected twists, and also having a lot of important lessons for us to absorb.

Conclusion

That's about everything there is to know about the book of Jonah. As you may have noticed, it's a pretty short story, but there's also a lot of depth to it. Not only are there a lot of different things that happen in the story, but there's also a ton of important information for us to absorb. Some of that information teaches us about the story, and some of it teaches us about God and how we should and shouldn't live our lives.

Jonah was a veteran prophet who was given a great opportunity to show us how we as children of God should live our lives, but he failed miserably. Everyone he encountered in this story, however, ended up serving as great examples for us to follow. In other words, we need to be more like the sailors and the Ninevites—who feared God and humbled themselves before him—and less like Jonah, who was biased, disobeyed God, and tried to run from God.

So many lessons in this short book

You may have noticed there are a lot of unexpected twists and turns throughout the book of Jonah that make it really interesting and entertaining to read. At the same time, you may have also noticed it has some very important lessons that we can take from it. One of the biggest is that we don't have to be perfect to be in a relationship with God or to be a servant of God. Anyone is capable of loving and serving God as long as they faithfully call Christ their one and only savior.

Even as God's children and servants, we all have flaws and can't do things on our own. It's imperative that we rely on God for help. He loves us, he's always there for us, he has a special plan for each of our lives, and we need to be ready to serve him when he calls us.

Another lesson we can take away from Jonah is that we can't avoid God by hiding and trying to do things on our own. Jonah showed us that it's not possible no matter how hard we try. We need to focus on staying close to God and be willing to serve him when he calls us into action. It's not a matter of *if* he'll call you, but *when* he'll call you. If you don't think you've heard him calling on you yet, you will eventually. If you've already experienced his calling you, don't be surprised if he does it again in your life so you can serve him in other ways.

It can be tempting to think you're not good enough for God because of your sins and your flaws, that there are others out there who are more equipped to serve him, but you need to remember that your sins and flaws are never too great for God. Look at how sinful the Ninevites were, yet God still loved them. He loves you, too, and he wants you to love him, serve him, and love others. He knows you're capable of doing that despite all your flaws.

Unfortunately, that can sometimes be hard for people to believe, and it can also be hard for them to try living with that type of mindset (it was definitely hard for Jonah to love the Ninevites). However, if you make an effort to view yourself more positively, not be biased toward others, and try to be more like Christ, you'll start feeling better about yourself and your capabilities; you'll start viewing others with an open mind and an open heart; and you'll also adopt a mindset centered around loving both God and the people in this world—people whom he also loves.

It may take some prayer and practice and maybe also some advice from others to adapt to these changes, but you're very much capable of it regardless of how you feel. When you do pull it off, you'll naturally adopt a much better image of both yourself and the people in your life, and you'll also have a much better relationship with them and with God.

Another lesson from Jonah is that we can't be selfish and want God's love to be just for us and maybe also a few others. That was another mistake Jonah made. God doesn't play favorites. He wants *everyone* to experience his love and mercy. He wants us to focus more on others than on ourselves. He doesn't want us to think the world revolves around us. It never has and it never will.

The fact that God loves *all* of us is another lesson we can take away from this book. It seems really simple, but it's important to fully understand it. He loves *all* of us and wants *all* of us to be saved. Despite all your sins and failures, he still loves you and wants you to follow him. It doesn't matter how sinful you are or how sinful you've been in the past, he still loves you and wants you to be in a relationship with him.

Since he doesn't play favorites, that means he doesn't want us to play favorites either. We can't be biased toward anyone in any sort of way. Jonah was obviously biased toward the Ninevites, and God didn't approve of that. God wants us to love everyone, regardless of who they are.

If we can all learn to love each other and serve God, this world will be a much more peaceful, uplifting, joyful, and united place. We'll all rejoice like the sailors in Jonah 1, we'll all humble ourselves like the Ninevites in Jonah 3, and we'll all live our lives to be more like Christ. That's what God wants us to do.

Adopting this mindset starts with each person individually. We each need to start by looking past our sins and the sins of others and understand that God is far greater than all our sins combined. There's no need to worry about our sins, because we're dead to them. Christ died on the cross so that all who believe in him can be free of their sins.

We then need to pray for guidance on how we should love others and serve God, and we need to be willing to move in that direction as soon as he shows us. We don't know God's plans for our lives, so we need to listen for his calling and trust him that that direction is the best one for us.

It's not good for us to take a guess at what God wants us to do. Without his guidance, things aren't going to work out for us, and God will find ways to move us away from that path and onto the one he wants us to follow. That's why we're better off waiting for him to call us. It may take some patience and prayer, but he's guaranteed call us at some point, and we need to be ready to act immediately.

There's a lot of work that God needs us to do in this broken world. Don't be like Jonah and waste your time and effort trying to hide from God while trying to do things on your own. It's a losing battle, and you're only delaying the inevitable while making your life, and sometimes also the lives of others, more difficult. You need to step up and say to him, "Here I am, Father. How can I serve you?" and when you find out what he wants you to do, your response needs to be, "Yes, Lord, I'll do it right away, and I'll do it to the best of my ability."

It may take some courage and faith for you to adopt this mindset (if you're struggling to do that, it never hurts to pray for the Holy Spirit to help you), but in the long run you'll be glad you did. In fact, God will also be glad you did, as well as those you end up helping while serving God. You may be surprised at how much you're able to accomplish and how much better you feel about your life. If you don't think it's possible, then not only do you need to have more trust in God (another thing you can pray for the Holy Spirit to give you) but you also need to remember Philippians 4:3, "I can do all things through [Christ] who gives me strength."

We each serve a purpose in this world, and that's part of the reason why God created us. If you haven't figured out yet what your purpose is, then it's time to ask God what it is and be ready to start serving once he shows you. Serving him should be the main focal point of our lives, and it should be done in love. The sooner you start living this way, the better. Your life may not necessarily become better, but deep down inside you'll have gained a sense of peace, fulfillment, satisfaction, and joy for what you're doing and what you've accomplished by serving God. Even better, you'll also be rewarded in heaven some day when you come face to face with Christ.

Don't just serve God and love others for his own sake, don't just do it for the sake of others, but do it for your own sake. You'll be glad you did, and some of you may even wish you had started doing that sooner. You may not reap the benefits here on earth, but you'll definitely reap the benefits in heaven for all eternity, which is what you should be striving for during your life on earth. Colossians 3:2 even says, "Set your minds on things above, not on earthly things."

The things on this earth will not last; they'll fade away (some more quickly than others) and become forgotten through time. However, doing things for God is eternal, and the rewards will be everlasting in heaven. Even if your acts of service toward him become forgotten on earth, they'll never be forgotten in heaven, where you'll someday be with God for all eternity. That is where you're guaranteed to be rewarded for serving him during your life on this earth.

This is not the time to ignore God, and it's definitely not the time to get distracted by the "plants" of this world either. He's waiting for you to step up and follow him. The longer you wait, the more likely your life is going to become very complicated, simply because God will be trying to get your attention. He won't stop until you've submitted yourself to him and are walking down the path he chose for you. Jonah's life became very complicated simply because he didn't listen to God. As a result, he encountered a vicious storm that forced him to be thrown overboard, and then he was eaten by a fish. God provided that storm and that fish to get Jonah's attention and to also draw Jonah back to him.

Symbolically speaking, if you're experiencing a vicious storm in your own life right now, then it's time to change your life around by turning to God and obeying his calling. Chances are he created that storm or at least allowed it to happen because you're doing something with your life that he doesn't want you to do. If you're doing something that you felt God has called you to do, and you encounter a storm, then it's possible God is using that storm to test you to see how faithful you are to him. If that's the case, then you need to be patient, continue to persevere, and ask God for help. You'll be able to recognize through prayer and discernment whether God is using that storm to test your faith or to make you change your direction in life, though sometimes it's more obvious than at others.

Remember that the life God has planned for you is the one you'll ultimately find most rewarding, especially in the long run. It might seem hard to believe at first, but that's where you really need to trust God. If you can do that and live the life he wants you to live, then someday, when you die and go to heaven, he'll say to you, "Well done, good and faithful servant."

That's an amazing reward we can to look forward to, and we'll receive it all because we chose to serve God. That's how important it is to God that we serve him. This world is full of sin and confusion, and it desperately needs to know about

Christ's sacrifice for our sins and about God's love and mercy. That message can be delivered through you, but you can't wait around to tell others about it. Everyone is going to die someday. If a person dies before being saved, it's too late for them. They're going to spend all eternity suffering in hell. You don't want that to happen to someone simply because you didn't feel like reaching out to them or because you made it a lower priority and your plan of reaching out to them got pushed back or forgotten. You might not get another opportunity, and if that person is someone you're close to, a friend or a family member, you're going to really regret missing that opportunity for the rest of your life. That's why it's so important for us to act now.

The opportunities for you to serve are already there, and there are many of them. Just ask God where to go and how he needs you to serve. Instead of running away like Jonah, or reluctantly obeying God like Jonah, or letting the "plants" of this world distract you like it did with Jonah, you need to focus on God and eagerly run toward his calling, knowing that your help is desperately needed and that it's also pleasing to God. Running toward him is easily your best and most rewarding option, and it's one of the few options in life you're guaranteed not to regret in the long run. The rewards will be eternal, and all because you did what God called you to do during your life on this earth.

That's how important it is to answer God's calling, and we learn about it, along with many other things we've already talked about, via a small book in the middle of the Bible called Jonah. It's sad to think this book sometimes gets overlooked by people who think it's not that important—that's it's just a kid-friendly story about a guy who gets swallowed and vomited by a fish. In fact, it's so short it can be easy to not even notice it when flipping through the pages in your Bible. However, there's a lot of information in this book that's very important for us to know about—not to mention that it's also an entertaining story with lots of interesting and unexpected twists and turns.

The book of Jonah is God's word, and this becomes obvious when you read it and notice the many connections it has with other books in the Bible. Like the other books of the Bible, God wants you to be fully aware of what it's about and how you can apply it to your life. He didn't have these books written just for fun; he had them written to help us in our spiritual lives.

There's no valid reason why you should ignore Jonah. Even now, after becoming familiar with it, the book has enough depth that you can easily go back and re-read it, study it, and pray about it, and you'll end up learning something new or be reminded of an important detail you may have forgotten. When you do this, you may even feel God calling you to serve him in a new way. If that happens, be ready to act, and do it willingly. That's the life God wants you to live, and it's the life you need to live. After all, not only are we his children, we're also his servants in a sinful and broken world that desperately needs our help. We should be a lot more concerned about the people in this world than about ourselves. We can help them, and even help ourselves along the way, by staying focused on God and serving him out of love.

Jonah didn't do that in this book, but we can learn from his mistakes and do a better job than him. God will be proud of us if we try. You may be surprised how much better you feel about yourself if you try, and you may be equally surprised by the impact you can have on the lives of others. That's how important we are to God, and what's better is that he's there to help us out. We're not alone in this journey. With him on our side, our potential is almost limitless.

It may seem pretty amazing how much depth there is to this short book in the Bible, but it shouldn't be when you think about it. God had this book written in the way he knew was best for us readers, and he had it written for very good reasons. It has also stood the test of time for very good reasons, so it's vital that you take it seriously, read it, learn from it, and apply it to your life. If you do that, you'll have the potential to become a much better person in God's eyes, and God will be able to do great things through you, even greater than you would've ever thought possible. You just need to trust in him, be open-minded, and be ready and willing to do whatever you feel he's calling you to do.

It may not always seem like it in the short run, but as time goes by, your decision to obey and serve God will become more and more rewarding in ways you didn't expect. You'll also be amazed at what you are able to accomplish over the years by following God and seeking his help. The rewards won't always be physically obvious here on Earth, but they'll definitely be spiritually obvious between you and God, and when you're in heaven someday you'll reap the benefits for all eternity.

That's a truly amazing experience we can look forward to. Until then, we have work to do here on Earth.

Clearly there are a plethora of things one can learn from the book of Jonah, despite it being so short. It's obviously much more than just a kid's story. It's the Word of God, and he had it written for our benefit.

About the Author

Chad Groen has an editorial background with multiple Christian book publishers. He has worked for Our Daily Bread Ministries as a copy editor and also for Zondervan as a proofreader. While working at Zondervan, he also wrote a devotion for the "New Men's Devotional Bible." He's been a Christian for most of his life and has gone to church his entire life. He and his wife Kristy are foster parents and live in Wyoming, Michigan, with their son, Zacchaeus.

Printed in the United States
by Baker & Taylor Publisher Services